D0046374

The Press in the Jury Box

HOWARD FELSHER
and MICHAEL ROSEN

THE PRESS
IN THE JURY BOX

THE MACMILLAN COMPANY · *NEW YORK*

First Printing

The Macmillan Company, New York

Collier-Macmillan Canada, Ltd., Toronto, Ontario

Library of Congress catalog card number: 66-10433

Printed in the United States of America

To

ALVIN PERLMUTTER,

for whom righteousness holds no terror

Acknowledgments

All the work involved in writing *The Press in the Jury Box* was made worthwhile by the reaction of friends to its premise. Few previously had recognized or even thought about the effect of newspaper and television reporting on jurors sitting in judgment on a defendant. Yet once they became aware that this factor could indeed have a negative bearing on our judicial system, they became sensitive to the appearance of such stories in the press. From that point onward, I had no fear that I would overlook a pertinent example. From all across the country, stories illustrating *The Press in the Jury Box* were mailed to me.

Particularly zealous in this regard were Mitchel and Gloria Levitas (themselves members of the Fourth Estate) and Dorianne and Roy Grutman (Dorianne, who works with the legal staff of the United Nations, provided me with information on the means other nations use to control this problem; Roy, an attorney, helped keep me abreast of legal thinking in this country). Eileen Za of Carnegie, Pennsylvania, sent reams of stories from Pittsburgh newspapers.

Lillian Pollock, whose years of editorial experience provided her with great expertise, gave of her advice willingly and of her approval grudgingly. The total of her advice and approval was of immeasurable help.

Writing a book while working full time at another occupation means nights and weekends stolen from one's family. To paraphrase a Navy wit, I gave this book one of the best years of my wife. Tex is her name, and I couldn't have known when I married her that events in her native state of Texas would occasion my first book. My six-year-old, Andy, lost uncountable weekends of play with his father. He has since exacted restitution.

No book of this sort could hope to be effective without the most thorough, exhaustive, and exhausting research. *The Press in the Jury Box* is no exception. Michael Rosen lived in law libraries, wrote hundreds of letters, and digested hundreds of cases to bring this book to the printed page. It is literally true that were it not for him, this book could not have been written.

Prentice-Hall, publisher of Irving Stone's *Earl Warren: A Great American Story* was most kind in granting permission to print excerpts from that book.

Finally, there is Herbert Lottman of Paris. Whatever merit this book has, it has because of his help. But where he is concerned, that is the story of my life.

The true measure of all these people is that they will consider themselves well thanked if *The Press in the Jury Box* provokes constructive comment.

HOWARD FELSHER

Contents

Preface

The problem of "trial by newspaper" is as old as the printing press. It has expanded now to include trial by magazine, radio, and television. There is no intention in these pages to single out newspapers for attack, for the wrongs discussed are committed by all communications media.

The authors salute the great and irreplaceable role played by the press in perpetuating our free society. Our free press exposes, informs, educates, and protects us. We could not do without it.

Yet all its utility does not make the press immune to criticism. Many have been the speeches and books that paid deserved tribute to the press. In the context of the present report, a tribute is not in order. But it is hoped that the press will realize that its contributions are not slighted by their omission from these pages.

The press is and should remain free. It will remain free even if all the recommendations we make in the following pages are adopted.

The Press in the Jury Box

PROLOGUE

Restraint, the Price of Liberty

G OD should have been a newspaperman. Then He would really be the focus of worship; He would lead a truly universal church. All the world prays to the power of the press.

This power is based on fear and the demonstrated ability of the press to mold the minds of men. The press makes or breaks. Huge corporations spend millions on oversized press-relations staffs. Presidents, senators, and town councilmen employ additional thousands of people to deal with the press. Governmental agencies, actors, stage and screen directors, police departments—even sanitation departments—all compete for coveted newspaper space. Magazines, newspapers, radio and TV stations—the press itself, incestuously, must have publicity to live.

The explanation is evident. Whatever the public knows about the events of the world, it knows only from newspaper, magazine, radio, and television accounts. What it reads or hears in the press, it is likely to believe. If the public believes the stories it reads in the press, it behooves those with stories to tell to get those stories into the press.

Yet only you and I use the press as a primary source of information. Governments have their embassies, their spy networks, their military missions, and whomever else they need on the scene where events occur. It is the full-time job of those agents to acquire the facts and to send them home to bulging file cabinets. Business, if it is big enough, has its own spies peering into the top-secret vaults of its competitors. The serious student depends on the historians.

For the public, there is only the press—and not much time to spend reading it, either. Decades after an event, one need only read a documented volume of history to realize how little truth was to be derived from the press at the time the event occurred. (This is not to say that the press was untruthful; rather, that it had access to only a tiny segment of the whole truth.)

Even in totalitarian countries, the public believes what it reads in the papers. Before Mao, the Chinese were friendly toward America and Americans. In less than ten years, that nation of six hundred million people has learned to hate us. This is true not only of the young Chinese, who are exposed to anti-Americanism in schools, but of the Chinese who have not been near a schoolroom in years, whose only contacts with the foreign world are newspapers and radio.

In this respect, we are not more privileged in America. Our bad habit is to accept the written word as gospel. How many arguments are settled by the statement "I saw it in the paper"? How many others are settled by a phone call to a local newspaper?

Press relations has become one of the big businesses in the world precisely because we are so strongly influenced by what we read and hear. It is not easy, despite our announced disdain, for any of us to dismiss a newspaper advertisement or a television commercial as propaganda. It is far harder when we read a newspaper story planted by a public-relations man. Ignorant of the reason for the story's appearance, we accept the story as news. It becomes part of the body of facts upon which we construct our opinions.

Inevitably, the first move of the leader of a *coup d'état* is against the press. If the press is free, he revokes its freedom. If it is or was faithful to the old regime, he shuts it down and begins anew.

Stalin, then Khrushchev, now Brezhnev, had *Pravda*. *Pravda* deified, then vilified Stalin. It began giving Khrushchev the latter treatment within days of his expulsion from power. Nowhere did we hear of disbelief on the part of the Russian readers. No one really knows with certainty just how gullible the Russian public is, but it seems likely that *Pravda*'s circulation would fall considerably if the public lost faith in it. Yet it remains the most important newspaper in Russia despite its zigzagging policies. Obviously, it represents a source of "truth" to its readers.

The process is the same in all the satellite countries. Even in heretical Yugoslavia, the press, while sometimes unfaithful to Moscow, is the faithful mistress of Tito.

No newspaper, magazine, or radio or TV station in Cuba opposes—or even criticizes—Fidel Castro. Little Paraguay has had a Stroessner press since General Alfredo Stroessner took over in 1954. Argentina's Juan Perón shocked the world when he closed *La Prensa*—one of the world's great newspapers. Hitler worked his way to power through manipulation of the press. De Gaulle, while not a complete dictator, has not hesitated to take measures against press and book publishers unfavorable to his position. And his political opponents find it impossible to get equal time on TV or radio, which are under state control in France. As a matter of fact, all of France once wondered when Henri Tisot, a satirical performer who found that De Gaulle was easily (and popularly) satirized, would wind up in jail. Even the balladeer "press" is dangerous to the ambitions of a dictator.

We are lost when our questions are answered by one source only. The press, whether it wants to or not, whether it admits to it or not, whether it accepts the responsibility or not, shapes our way of life.

This being the case, it would seem that the press of this country would impose upon itself a code of ethics far stronger than the golden rule. There is no quarrel with the claim of the publishers that a free press is the cornerstone of democracy. Yet, unless it exercises a great deal more self-restraint, the press will find itself responsible for the weakening of that democracy.

There are few more painful examples than those in the McCarthy era. Certainly, Senator Joseph McCarthy would have been no more of a nuisance than a sterile flea had not his accusations been stamped across the face of the nation in headlines indelible to this day. There were few newspapers in this land that chose to weigh his charges, or to confine them to inside pages until verification was forthcoming. The bulk of the press brought out its biggest type, its loudest commentators, to scare us all into believing that the Russians were perched on the three-mile limit. We lost some of our ablest diplomats, reviled some of our finest writers, expelled many excellent schoolteachers, questioned the patriotism of our greatest scientists. And too late we discovered that McCarthyism was a madness.

There were people who wouldn't eat borscht for fear of the consequences. One State Department man—part of whose job it was to read the *Daily Worker* reached the ludicrous extreme of hiding his personal copy of the New York *Post* underneath the *Worker*, because the *Post* had been attacked by Senator McCarthy.

Anything or anyone McCarthy attacked was named in the press. The attack was sufficient; people stopped at the headline. By abdicating its clear responsibility to print only the truth, by not taking the trouble to try to verify charges before printing them, by not even waiting until someone else verified them, the press became as responsible for McCarthyism as McCarthy himself was. Much of the press editorialized against McCarthy. But that happened on the back pages. The front pages continued to headline the McCarthy assault.

In its eagerness to run headlines, the press fell back on a most primitive concept of what is news. An officeholder—a senator of the United States—speaks. Ergo, it is news. Because the press accepted this concept, the constitutional rights of some American citizens were compromised by the constitutionally safeguarded free press.

Another more understandable but equally unfortunate example of the power of the press to crush the Constitution dates back to December 8, 1941, the day after Pearl Harbor. We had every legitimate reason to hate the Japanese leadership for its treachery. However, the Japanese leadership was six thousand miles away. The counterattack of organized public opinion was directed not only against the Japanese war machine, but against thousands of unfortunate individuals who lived on our own West Coast—Japanese-Americans (the Nisei) who should have been assumed to be good American citizens.

West Coast newspapers churned up a frenzy of fear. Immediately after Pearl Harbor, California newspapers quoted

Secretary of War Frank Knox on the sabotage at that base as "the most effective fifth-column work that's come out of this war, except in Norway."

Headlines read: FIFTH COLUMN PREPARED ATTACK, FIFTH COLUMN TREACHERY TOLD, SECRETARY OF NAVY BLAMES FIFTH COLUMNISTS FOR THE RAID.

These newspapers also printed a story describing how worried Californians had plowed under "a beautiful field of flowers on the property of a Japanese farmer" because they thought "the Jap was a fifth columnist and had grown his flowers in a way that, when viewed from a plane, formed an arrow pointing the direction to the airport."

Other completely unfounded stories announced that Japanese submarines operating right off the West Coast had fired on American shipping, that the West Coast was virtually blockaded.

United Press correspondent Wallace Carrol dispatched a story reading:

Japanese of American nationality infiltrated in the police departments and obtained jobs as road supervisors, sanitary inspectors or minor government officials. Many went to work in the post office and telephone service, ideal posts for spies. . . .

An American resident, who had studied Japanese methods in Manchuria and North China, told me that the Japanese fifth column and espionage organizations in the islands were similar to those which had been used to undermine the Chinese.

The San Diego *Union* editorialized:

In Hawaii and in the Philippines treachery by residents, who although of Japanese ancestry had been regarded by us as loyal, has played an important part in the success of the Japanese attacks. . . .

Every Japanese—for the protection of those who are loyal to us and those who are not—should be removed out of the coastal area and to a point of safety far enough inland to nullify any inclination they may have to tamper with our safety here.

Just a few days later, the same newspaper renewed its demand:

We are confronted on both sides by enemies who have devoted their entire careers to the development of treachery, deceit and sabotage. We can afford to be neither soft-headed nor soft-hearted in dealing with them or their agents.

Henry McLemore, filing from Los Angeles for the Hearst papers, wrote in his column:

The only Japanese apprehended have been the ones the F.B.I. actually had something on. The rest of them, so help me, are free as birds. There isn't an airport in California that isn't flanked by Japanese farms. There is hardly an air field where the same situation doesn't exist. . . .

I know this is the melting pot of the world and all men are created equal and there must be no such thing as race or creed hatred, but do these things go when this country is fighting for its life? Not in my book. No country has ever won a war because of courtesy and I trust and pray we won't be the first because of the lovely, gracious spirit. . . .

I am for immediate removal of every Japanese on the West Coast to a point deep in the interior. I don't mean a nice part of the interior either. Herd 'em, pack 'em off and give 'em the inside room in the bad lands. Let 'em be pinched, hurt, hungry and dead up against it. . . .

Personally, I hate the Japanese. And that goes for all of them.

Walter Lippmann, the voice of reason in our newspaper world, wrote:

The Pacific Coast is officially a combat zone; some part of it may at any moment be a battlefield. Nobody's constitutional rights include the right to reside and do business on a battlefield. . . . There is plenty of room elsewhere for him to exercise his rights.

The San Francisco *Examiner:*

EX-POLICE CHIEF OF TOKYO HELD BY FBI IN RAID ON SALINAS

The San Francisco *News:*

The Japanese proprietor of a sporting goods store possessed 70,000 rounds of rifle and shotgun ammunition, 12 rifles and shotguns, a public address system, camera and film, books of Japanese propaganda and a radio operator's handbook.

Chief Justice of the United States Earl Warren, then Attorney-General of California, was quoted in the Monterey *Press Herald* as stating that the Japanese situation "may well be the Achilles heel of the entire civilian defense effort. Unless something is done, it may bring about a repetition of Pearl Harbor."

Special praise, though, must go to the San Francisco *Chronicle.* Only six weeks after Pearl Harbor, it published a front-page editorial calling for nondiscrimination against Japanese-Americans and deprecating plans for mass evacuation.

Its voice was a voice alone.

Because the press was so pervasive, so one-sided, we became frightened enough to permit our government to send these Japanese-Americans to concentration camps without charges, investigations, or defense. On the surface, they looked to be "Japanese." Thus, they were also the enemy, and a clear and present danger.

Admittedly, our newspapers did not bring about Pearl Harbor. But neither did our Japanese-Americans. Our newspapers *did* provoke a nationwide hatred of all Japanese through their catchall campaign of vilification, which did not bother to distinguish between the Japanese of Japan and Americans of Japanese ancestry. Such was the power of the press that constitutional rights, supposedly enjoyed by all Americans, were abridged for some.

Fortunately, large groups can usually fight back. So many Americans were painted pink, so many Nisei were branded traitorous, that great segments of the population rebelled and awakened the conscience of the nation.

There is no way of fighting back, though, when the press gangs up on an individual. It is in the area of individual liberties that the press most needs examination. In this area, it may be aggressive, even barbaric. Privacy, pride, dignity—anything that helps a person hold up his head can be destroyed by the press in search of a story. Sometimes it is worse. If the sensational press has a possible criminal to work over, its irresponsibility knows no bounds. There is no estimating the number of persons sent to prison because they were convicted, before trial, by the press. That is our concern in this book.

The press can overwhelm and then destroy an individual's right to a fair trial by reporting inflammatory details about the suspect and the crime before he is ever brought to trial. Assuming that most people read newspapers and listen to radio and TV, and that most of them follow sensational crime news with somewhat more eagerness than they read the stock tables, it becomes more and more difficult to find potential jurors who have no knowledge of, and hence no bias toward, the defendant.

The Constitution guarantees the right to a fair trial. It also guarantees the right to a free press. These two rights collide when a sensational crime is committed, and the collision often wrecks the chances of the defendant's finding an impartial jury.

The press cries, "The public has a right to know." Lawyers reply, "The defendant has a right to a fair trial." But the *status quo* remains, and the verdicts become matters for appeals courts to weigh. What appeals court can know whether or not a jury was impartial? Clearly it is time for us to ask whether freedom of the press includes the right to abridge the constitutional rights of others.

Our history as a nation is filled with examples of constitutionally guaranteed rights colliding with each other. Happily, there are almost as many examples of something being done about it. The huge proliferation of governmental regulatory agencies is testimony to the need for adjusting the contradictions between human rights and property rights; this adjusting is a continual process. Constitutionally, there was nothing illegal about a laissez-faire economy. In human terms, there was a lot wrong with it. So government stepped in, used its power to interpret the Constitution, and determined that if each of the aggrieved parties could claim to have the Constitution on its side, the inside track would be awarded to the individual.

The Securities and Exchange Commission, the Pure Food and Drug Administration, the Federal Power Commission, the Federal Trade Commission, the Interstate Commerce Commission, the Federal Communications Commission, and the Federal Reserve Board are all examples of bureaucracy created to protect the rights of the individual by limiting the rights of groups far stronger than any one of us. There are, too, protective laws like the Sherman and Clayton acts. Outside the federal government, all the states and every municipality worth the name have gone in the same direction. States and cities regulate insurance companies, hospitals, construction, education, banking, local health problems, and many other areas of potential conflict peculiar to the local situation.

Each of these agencies bridles the freedom of an enterprise, or group of enterprises, in order to protect individuals from freedom gone rapacious.

There was a time, remembered by many still alive, when *caveat emptor* was the standard gauge of business ethics. If the buyer was not intelligent enough to see through a fraud, it was his hard luck. In the securities field, for example, there were no limits on the content of advertising used to sell stocks and bonds. It was easy to misrepresent, to convolute the truth, to hide facts or twist them to make a sale. This was picnic-time for the robber barons. They recognized long before Barnum did that a sucker is born every minute, and they made sure that few of the newborn would grow to old age without deserving that label.

The stock market was an easy place to fool the public. Financial statements were (and still are) hard to understand; promises were easy to make and there was no law requiring that they be kept. The results, of course, were unpredictable but manipulated rises and falls in stock prices, with hundreds of thousands of individuals losing hundreds of millions of dollars.

The Federal Securities Act, enforced by the Securities and Exchange Commission, has changed this by refusing to consider false claims for a stock as "freedom of speech." Freedom of speech, of course, is one of our basic freedoms. We are constantly reminded that without complete freedom of speech, we cannot have any freedom at all. Yet we have denied "freedom" to dishonest dealers to "speak" falsely about their wares—and still we remain, as a nation, as democratic as ever.

Thirty or more years ago, Mr. Carl D. Shaefer would have had no laws to worry about in connection with raising money for the manufacture of a steam-making machine he invented. There was then no Federal Securities Act making it unlawful in the offer or sale of securities to obtain money or property by means of any untrue statement of a material fact or any omission of a material fact. Mr. Shaefer could legally have spoken out to his heart's content.

Mr. Shaefer claimed he had invented a machine that would create steam from practically nothing. Steam is one of the world's great sources of power. Millions upon millions of tons of coal are used to manufacture steam; equal millions of gallons of oil, tons of wood, and who knows how much uranium are used for the same purpose. Mr. Shaefer claimed that his machine was so good, so economical, that it would make even atomic power obsolete because it needed so little energy to work up a full head of steam.

Apparently he had no difficulty in convincing investors of the merits of his machine. He raised more than two million dollars from several hundred investors partially because of the revolutionary implications of his invention. In fact, even after he was brought to court, the worth of his machine was never in question.

However, the quality of his invention was not the only criterion the investors used in deciding to invest. There is a commercial aphorism that warns, "When you're investing, be sure you have someone else to lean on." In other words, before putting money into a project, make sure someone else is taking the same gamble.

Shaefer must have run head on into that aphorism. He was brought to court by several investors who charged that he falsely told them that Dow Chemical Company, du Pont, Chrysler and General Motors were so taken by his machine that they had formed a syndicate to purchase it, and to that end had put ten million dollars in escrow in the Chase National Bank in New York. He further told them, they charged, that Fairbanks, Morse and Company, and the Crane Company had each offered one million dollars for the machine, and that the U.S. Navy also wanted to buy it.

Shaefer, who three decades earlier would have had no fear of legal difficulties about these misrepresentations—this "freedom of speech"—was found guilty of violating the Federal Securities Act. By denying Shaefer, and others like him, freedom to falsify, the law protects individual investors.

Since Carl Shaefer was guilty of outright lying, it would seem that his freedom of speech was properly curtailed. Who, after all, should be permitted to lie? Luckily these safeguards, these abridgments of freedom of speech, apply against innuendo as well as against deliberate falsehood.

The Federal Trade Commission Act makes it unlawful to disseminate false advertisements by any means for the purpose of inducing, directly or indirectly, the purchase of food, drugs, devices, or cosmetics. In 1962, the Federal Trade Commission took the Bakers Franchise Corporation to court, charging it with false advertisements in violation of the act.

In 1962, we had become a nation of waistline watchers. Low-calorie foods erupted, literally, out of the earth. Thousands of science-fiction-like experiments were inflicted on our plant life to deprive it of its natural heritage, to make it non-

fattening even as it came up out of the ground. For a fortunately short time, we forgot our preoccupation with the
bosom to concentrate on the belly (the emphasis is shifting
back where it belongs). People who couldn't add two and two
were counting calories, subtracting calories, multiplying calories. We were on our way to becoming a nation of wizened
wizards.

The conditions were perfect for an assault on the American
consumer. It was not long in coming. Low-calorie drinks, no-
calorie candy, nonfattening ice cream became available
everywhere. Clothing manufacturers tuned up their sewing
machines to make new clothes to cover the new, trim, stream-
lined American. About the only industry unable to take advantage of the new look of life was the tobacco industry—the
one industry whose product could really lay claim to reducing
the appetite. Unfortunately for it, if it were to be candid, it
would also have to lay claim to reducing life itself. (Herein,
incidentally, is a perfect example of the ambiguity of our love
for freedom of speech. The government wants cigarette manufacturers to print on their packages a warning about the
health dangers of cigarettes. The tobacco industry is totally
opposed. This kind of freedom of speech is too much for the
tobacco industry.)

For vanity or for health, as a nation, we were ready to
listen to the promises of those who would trim us.

Enter the Bakers Franchise Corporation with its secret formula for the manufacture of Lite Diet bread. Local bakeries
across the country bought franchises to bake and distribute
Lite Diet bread, using the formula of the parent company.
The parent company also supplied the advertising campaign
to promote the sale of the bread. They ran several ads.
"Who'd believe it could help control your weight? So try

it—Lite Diet—Lite Diet—Lite Diet." And "Here's a bread that tastes great yet helps you control weight. It's Lite Diet, Lite Diet, Lite Diet." And "Will you listen to him? Says it helps you keep slim—do try it—Lite Diet, Lite Diet." And "Who'd ever think such delicious bread could help keep you slim?"

The Federal Trade Commission charged that these ads were an attempt to tell the public that eating Lite Diet was a good way to keep from gaining weight.

Bakers Corporation, in its defense (which, unbelievably enough, it presented with a straight face), pointed out that Lite Diet was *sliced* thinner than ordinary bread, that consequently a slice of it contained fewer calories than an ordinary slice. This was true. The F.T.C., though, fought back by saying that, pound for pound, Lite Diet had the same number of calories as any other bread. This, too, was true.

Thus there was no real misstatement of fact. Bakers Franchise Corporation had never lied in its advertisements. Yet the court affirmed the finding of the Federal Trade Commission. Bakers Corporation advertising was deceptive— deception achieved by innuendo rather than by outright falsehoods. Again, the individual consumer's rights had been protected by the curtailment of Bakers Corporation's right of freedom to speak and in so doing to deceive.

In 1964 alone, our state and federal regulatory agencies interceded in hundreds of conflicts to protect the interests of the individual. The Civil Aeronautics Board forced lower air fares; the F.C.C. upheld the equal-time ruling, to allow minority-party candidates a chance to have their say. New York City's Commissioner of Markets investigated retail establishments that were overcharging consumers, New York State's Public Service Commission denied railroad fare increases, a criminal information was returned against a large New York department store for false advertising.

In all these cases, and hundreds more, when the rights of the individual were in conflict with the rights of property, the individuals were defended by government agencies— government agencies that had been legislated into existence to fill a need, to right wrongs.

This principle—and it is a vital principle—could similarly be applied to the press in its treatment of crime news. Since the press continues to demonstrate that it will not, or cannot, protect the rights of the individual in reporting crime, we must decide how these rights can be protected in the context of the Constitution. Is a man accused, but not convicted, of burglary, or even murder, less deserving of his constitutional rights than a weight-conscious housewife?

Nowhere are newspapers so thorough as they are in reporting crimes. The bloodier the crime, the more specific the report. Let the crime be bloody and disgusting at the same time and there is no predicting the amount of space it will get in the papers. A narcotics murder is worth a half-dozen hit-and-run deaths to an editor with a sense of reader interest. Rape is a headline; rape plus perversion plus throat-cutting is the approach of the millennium.

When a suspect in a sensational case is finally picked up and booked, editors may well lay in an extra supply of ink. Every detail of the crime is re-created, every scar on the suspect's face is lengthened and colored; the arresting officers are besieged for quotes (and usually give them), investigating officers are asked what evidence they have (and usually give it), school records are examined, employers questioned, and families badgered. The crudest behavior is piously justified by editorial affirmations of the public's right to know.

In crime reporting, the press prints every fact it can find, and some facts it imagines. We read the stories and prejudge the defendant before he has been near the courtroom.

At some point during the time we were borrowing our judicial system from the English, we closed our eyes and missed the guarantee of the rights of the accused with regard to the press. The English long ago recognized that the press, if it would have a conscience at all, would have it only if imposed by law. They forbade the press to publish pertinent details of a crime, or information about the defendant, until after the trial. This is not to say that the English press is not free. It is. But its freedom is not utilized to compromise a defendant's right to a fair trial. The English press can publish everything it wants to publish—after the trial. But the trial cannot be fair if potential jurors have been conditioned to hate. In America, unhappily, the defendant does not have that protection.

Today, there are many who advocate a choke collar on unlimited license to report crime news. When custom denies a defendant the full protection of due process of law, that custom must be re-examined.

If other rights, discussed earlier in this chapter, have been interpreted in behalf of the individual by regulatory agencies, it seems not undemocratic to suggest that legislators must now take a stand to curtail the excesses of the press against the person accused of a crime. The depth of the problem and its contradictory aspects are illustrated by two briefs filed in a case known as the *Baltimore Radio Show v. State of Maryland*, in the Maryland Court of Appeals in 1949. Each brief was filed as "a friend of the court." Each was filed by a civil liberties group. One brief argued that the right of fair trial was

most important. The other argued that freedom of the press
was paramount.

Many legislators are aware of the dilemma. Some even suggest doing something about it. So do a few judges. The Brook-
ings Institution of Washington, D.C., is undertaking a major
study of the problem. Dr. Frank Stanton, president of C.B.S.,
has publicly recognized the dangers. Newspaper editors are
still to be heard from. Even so magnificent an editor as Turner
Catledge of the New York *Times* refuses to concede that the
press will not regulate itself.

Justice Bernard S. Meyer, of the Supreme Court of New
York, one of the leaders in the fight for press regulation, puts
the entire problem succinctly when he says, "One of the
judge's grudges is the press's excesses."

Judge Hubert L. Will, of the U. S. District Court for the
Northern District of Illinois, points out that freedom of the
press is even now not an unqualified, absolute right; that it is
subject to restrictions in certain areas. He said, "Confidential
government documents, for example, however newsworthy,
are not the legitimate subject of complete press inquiry. Disclosure to the press of information not open to the public
generally could seriously undermine the various branches of
government. . . . Thus, restraint on the press has sound reason
to support it, reasons to which much of the press itself sub-
scribes. It should be added, of course, that control of allegedly
classified information may be subject to abuses by the government, but in this realm of constitutional conflict, over-all balance decidedly favors the government's interest over that of
'freedom of the press.' "

Judge Alexander Holtzoff, U. S. District Judge for the District of Columbia, was even more specific at a conference on
"Fair Trial and Freedom of the Press." He said:

Fundamentally, the problem grows out of the fact that the various privileges guaranteed by the Bill of Rights are not entirely unrelated, unqualified, or unlimited. They do not operate in a vacuum. They frequently impinge and encroach on one another. It becomes necessary, therefore, to find and steer a true course, and to maintain a balance that would accord to each of these rights its due, and yet would not adversely affect any other. For example, many years ago when it was attempted to justify polygamy as an exercise of the freedom of religion guaranteed by the First Amendment, the Supreme Court held that freedom of religion does not extend to the commission of acts regarded by society as immoral and made criminal by law. To take another well-known example, an outstanding liberal [Justice Oliver Wendell Holmes] once remarked that the right of freedom of speech does not justify a person getting up in a crowded theater and shouting, "Fire!"

Walter Lippmann, on the same subject, said, "I am unable to believe that the press would be less free if some reasonable restraint were put upon the right to make instantaneous copy out of clues which are vital to the detection of crime."

Judge James S. Bell, of the Supreme Court of Ohio, began his opinion in Dr. Sam Sheppard's appeal from a murder conviction with these words:

Murder and mystery, society, sex and suspense were combined in this case in such a manner as to intrigue and captivate the public fancy to a degree perhaps unparalleled in recent annals. Throughout the preindictment investigation, the subsequent legal skirmishes and the nine-week trial, circulation-conscious editors catered to the insatiable interest of the American public in the bizarre. Special seating facilities for reporters and columnists representing local papers and all major news services were installed in the courtroom. Special rooms in the Criminal Courts building were equipped for broadcasters and telecasters. In this atmosphere of a "Roman

Holiday" for the news media, Sam Sheppard stood trial for his life.

Perhaps, though, as might be expected, it was H. L. Mencken who said it best. "The much needed purge of journalism must be accomplished by external forces, and through the medium of penalties exteriorly inflicted."

All these responsible men are concerned about the dangers inherent in the crime reporting of an irresponsible press. The major dangers and an effort at their solution will be found in succeeding chapters.

ONE

The Brain as Sponge

THE "twelve good men and true" who are the jury in a criminal trial have no special training to qualify them for their seats. No more than being a woman means that you will automatically be a good mother does being a citizen guarantee that you will be a good juror.

One does not set aside opinions of a lifetime, prejudices etched in a brain, because one steps into a courtroom to determine the fate of a defendant. Just as it is impossible to ignore one's own attitudes, it is equally impossible to ignore facts (or purported facts) about a case about to be tried. The brain has an infinite capacity to absorb. Much of what is absorbed is subject to recall.

Newspaper accounts and television broadcasts about a crime spring back to mind while you are sitting on a jury. You cannot dismiss them just because the judge has told you that you must.

Judges, recognizing these potential dangers, attempt to alleviate them in their pre-trial instructions to the jury. Before a trial begins the judge outlines to the jury what it can and cannot do. An integral part of those instructions is a direct

[35]

order to disregard anything read or heard about the case, to make decisions solely on the evidence to be given in the courtroom, and *not to read* the press or watch television news stories about the case.

Justice Bernard S. Meyer of the Supreme Court of the State of New York always includes in his instructions to the jury this exhortation:

During the time you serve on this jury there may appear in the newspapers or on radio or television broadcasts reports concerning the trial and you may be tempted to read or listen to or watch them. *Please do not do so.* The process of law requires that the evidence to be considered by you in reaching your verdict meet certain standards, as for example that a witness testify only about facts that he has himself seen or heard rather than what was told to him by others and that he be subject to cross-examination.

The information media are not governed by such standards in what they present. If you read, listen to, or watch such reports of this trial, matters which could not be presented to you in this courtroom may reach you, and the defendant would have no chance to test it or respond to it.

In fairness to the defendant, therefore, it is important that you pay strict attention to this admonition not to read, listen to, or watch any such report. [italics added]

Justice Meyer maintains, though, that his charge can do nothing about information previously absorbed. Psychologists agree with him. Justice Meyer believes that members of many juries are irremediably prejudiced against the defendant before they have heard a word of testimony.

Simon H. Rifkind, former United States District Judge for the Southern District of New York and today a leading attorney in private practice, has commented:

To exclude from the jury panel all who have read about the case or heard about it over the radio is to reduce the jury to the blind, the deaf, and the illiterate. So the jury must be selected from these precharged human vessels.

Justice Meyer, adding to Judge Rifkind's remarks, has said:

If a confession has been read in the newspapers, or heard about on television, I doubt very seriously that any human being can cast it out of his mind. Therefore, an instruction to do so will have very little effect. There's at least one picturesque jurist who at one point said that to give such an instruction is like telling a young child to stand in the corner and not to think about a white elephant. Obviously he can't think about anything else.

I do not believe that there is any corrective measure— instructions to the jury, new trial, moving the trial, bringing in jurors from elsewhere, locking the jury up, that can effectively do away with the prejudice once it has occurred.

Therefore the only way to deal with it is to prevent it from occurring in the first place.

Circuit Court Judge Calvert Magruder said:

One cannot assume that the average juror is so endowed with a sense of detachment, so clear in his introspective perception of his own mental processes, that he may confidently exclude even the unconscious influence of his preconceptions as to probable guilt, engendered by a pervasive pretrial publicity.

One significant fact about the preceding statements is that they were all made by judges, men who have gone beyond the battleground before the bench and now sit as impartial observers. They are the men who must administer justice. They no longer take sides. They are not advocates for the prosecution or the defense. They care only about impartiality and fairness. These judges who decry trial by newspaper have found, through their own experience, that the brain is a very absorbent sponge.

When the United States prosecuted a defendant named Juelich for murder, all twelve jurors impaneled in the case admitted on *voir dire* (the pre-trial examination of prospective jurors by the court) that they had already formed opinions that the defendant was guilty on the basis of newspaper stories and newscasts. Despite this admission, they maintained that they could disregard their opinions if called as jurors, that they would render a verdict based only on the evidence admitted in the trial itself. Inexplicably, they were seated as jurors. . . . Juelich was found guilty of murder.

The U.S. Court of Appeals reversed the conviction, holding, in *Juelich v. United States,* that the lower court was in error to try a defendant before such a jury. The court, too, seemed convinced that once an opinion is formed it cannot be discarded.

In most instances of an affirmation of conviction, the jurors in the original trial, though admitting that they had read newspaper accounts, claimed that they had not formed opinions based on those accounts. Hence the appeals courts were able to hold that pre-trial publicity had not made a fair trial impossible. In *Juelich v. United States* the jurors admitted they *had* formed opinions, but maintained they could ignore them. Obviously the appeals court was not willing to accept so illogical a position. It did not believe that they had really been able to set aside the opinions they held at the start of the trial. It is thus clear that our courts believe that "admitted" opinions can be stronger than real evidence.

The danger to a defendant lies with those jurors who do not admit to their preconceived opinions. And, unless they are the "blind, the deaf, and the illiterate," they do have opinions.

There is an additional distinction, made by the United States Supreme Court in *Marshall v. United States*. Howard R. Marshall was arrested for unlawfully dispensing certain drugs without a prescription. During his trial the government attempted to introduce evidence to show that he had been convicted several years earlier of practicing medicine without a license. The judge refused to admit the evidence into testimony as being prejudicial and having no bearing on the present case. Despite the judge's ruling, the *Rocky Mountain News* published the following story:

Marshall has a record of two previous felony convictions. In 1953, while serving a forgery sentence in the State Penitentiary at McAlester, Oklahoma, Marshall testified before a state legislative committee studying new drug laws for Oklahoma.

At that time, he told the committee that although he had only a high school education, he practiced medicine with a $25 diploma he received through the mails. He told in detail of the ease in which he wrote and passed prescriptions for dangerous drugs.

The Denver *Post*, not to be outdone, went further in its story:

The defendant was Howard R. (Tobey) Marshall, once identified before a committee of the Oklahoma legislature as a man who acted as a physician and prescribed restricted drugs for Hank Williams before the country singer's death in December, 1953. . . .

Marshall was arrested with his wife, Edith Every Marshall, 56, in June, 1956. She was convicted on the drug charges in Federal District Court here in November and was sentenced to 60 days in jail.

Records show that Marshall once served a term in the Oklahoma penitentiary for forgery. There is no evidence he is a doctor, court attaches said.

Seven of the twelve jurors admitted to seeing these articles. All seven protested that they had not been prejudiced by them. Marshall was convicted.

His attorneys appealed to the U.S. Supreme Court. The court ordered a new trial. It held that evidence so prejudicial that it was ruled inadmissible by the trial judge should not have come, through other means, to the attention of the jurors.

Again, the court affirmed its belief that information soaked up by the brain could not be squeezed out. The distinction here, of course, is that the information printed by the two newspapers had been ruled inadmissible by the judge. This circumstance is not found in most instances when the court upholds a conviction.

Many people are not even aware that they can be influenced adversely by newspaper stories. One prospective juror, who obviously hoped or anticipated that he would be called to sit in judgment on Dr. Sam Sheppard, deliberately read the newspapers in Cleveland to learn more about the case. During his examination on *voir dire* he said he had read about the case daily after he learned that his name was on the list of veniremen (prospective jurors), "because if I were chosen I'd know something about the case." (Give that person credit for good intentions, no matter how misguided.)

Determine for yourself whether or not it was possible to forget or ignore the facts printed before the trial in the case of *Leslie Irvin v. Dowd*, in Indiana.

In 1955, the state of Indiana was horrified and frightened by six murders committed near Evansville. The authorities arrested Leslie Irvin on suspicion of murder. Shortly after the arrest, and before Irvin was indicted, the prosecutor issued press releases announcing that Irvin had confessed to the six murders. The newspapers printed the releases. As a result of the prosecutor's statement the entire state of Indiana must have formed the opinion that Irvin was the murderer.

Some of the headlines in the local press, published before the indictment, follow:

Evansville *Press*:

IRVIN PLACED AT MURDER SCENE: REPORTED SEEKING TO MAKE DEAL

CAR SEEN TURNING INTO DUNCAN LANE [Three members of the Duncan family were murder victims.]

Evansville *Courier* (front page):

SIX MURDERS SOLVED!
REPORT DETAILS OF HOW KILLINGS WERE EXECUTED

The rest of the front page, all the rest, was devoted to macabre details of the six killings, telling, in each of the six cases, how Irvin purportedly killed the victims.

Evansville *Press*:

ADMITTED KILLER OF SIX AREA PERSONS SPENDS 25 MINUTES TALKING WITH PRIEST
WHAT MADE IRVIN A KILLER?

Evansville *Courier*:

MASS-KILLER LESLIE IRVIN BARES DETAILS OF SIX AREA SLAYINGS TO LOCAL POLICE
CONFESSIONS END SIX-DAY SILENCE

It was *after* these headlines and stories were printed that Irvin was indicted. Several days before his trial began, this story appeared in the *Courier*:

Police who arrested him say Irvin has confessed to six murders in two states, ranging over a period of four months, and the convicted burglar will go on trial Monday for only one, in Evansville. . . .

In oral statements given police after his arrest, Irvin said he first slugged Mrs. Holland into unconsciousness, then shot her in the head when she came to and screamed as he was taking money from the store. . . .

He said he shot Kerr, attendant at a service station on the corner of U.S. 41 and Franklin Street, and robbed the station after talking with the 20-year-old father of three from 10 P.M. to 1 A.M. Dec. 23, 1954. . . .

The day before the trial began, the *Courier*, again:

Evansville police say Irvin has orally admitted the Kerr slaying; the robbery-murder of Mrs. Mary Holland; the murder of Mrs. Wilhelmina Sailer in Posey County and the slaughter of three members of the Duncan family in Henderson County, Ky.

Then, on the day the trial began, the Evansville *Press* reported:

Leslie Irvin, who has admitted to police that he shot six persons to death to cover up three petty larcenies, pleaded innocent.

When Irvin's case came to trial his attorney moved for a change of venue, citing the extensive, damaging pre-trial publicity as his reason. The motion was granted, but the trial was moved only to a nearby community which had itself been treated to huge amounts of publicity concerning the case.

At that point the trial became a local *cause célèbre*. One newspaper assigned a reporter to rove the streets to find out how many people thought Irvin was guilty and to ask these people what punishment to give Irvin. The results of the survey (Irvin was "guilty") were published in the newspapers and broadcast on radio and television.

Irvin's attorney moved for another change of venue. In court he produced forty-six exhibits to demonstrate that a fair trial would be impossible. All the exhibits were newspaper stories, headlines, cartoons, and photographs.

The newspapers carrying the stories had reached 95% of the homes in Gibson County, Indiana, the county where Irvin was to go on trial for his life. If 5 per cent of the homes had missed the newspapers, the omission was remedied by the Evansville radio and television stations. Their newscasts and special broadcasts covered the same stories in the same detail.

They told that Irvin had committed crimes while still a juvenile, that twenty years before these murders he had been convicted on an arson charge, and again for burglary, that an Army court-martial had convicted him on AWOL charges, and, finally, that he was a parole violator.

They said, too, that Irvin had been identified in a police line-up, that he had been identified at the scene of the crime (he was on trial for only one of the murders), that, in fact, the murders were solved but Irvin refused to confess.

Then they announced that he had finally confessed, and had also offered to plead guilty in return for a ninety-nine-year sentence instead of the death penalty. The prosecutor, however, was determined to get the death penalty. The newspapers printed that, too.

There were additional stories reporting that Irvin had confessed to twenty-four robberies. The writers went on to compare the details of those robberies with the details of the murders, pointing out that there were more than coincidental similarities. These stories were never fully substantiated in fact.

One newspaper ran a dramatic interview with a Kentucky sheriff who promised to "devote his life to getting Irvin executed by Kentucky if Indiana didn't do it first." Another characterized Irvin as "remorseless" and "without conscience," but added that he had been found sane by a court-appointed panel of doctors.

Most of the stories described Irvin as a "confessed slayer of six," a "parole violator," and a "fraudulent-check artist."

There were 430 people on the panel of veniremen—430 from among whom only twelve had to be selected as jurors. Within two days of the beginning of the selection process newspapers reported that "strong feelings, often bitter and angry, rumbled to the surface" of the veniremen as lawyers questioned them, and that "the extent to which the multiple murders—three in one family—have aroused feelings throughout the area was emphasized on Friday, when twenty-seven of the thirty-five prospective jurors questioned were excused for holding biased pre-trial opinions."

A few days later stories described the feeling as "a pattern of deep and bitter prejudice against the former pipe fitter." Other stories printed comments by spectators in the courtroom: "My mind is made up," "I think he is guilty," and "He should be hanged."

The trial itself had not begun. Irvin, supposedly, still lived under a presumption of innocence.

Finally, after many days of attempts to select jurors, a newspaper headline discovered:

IMPARTIAL JURORS ARE HARD TO FIND

That might be the funniest headline of all time. Of the 430 prospective jurors, 268 were excused by the court itself because they admitted having fixed opinions concerning Irvin's guilt. Another 103 were excused because they opposed the death penalty. Irvin's counsel challenged twenty more (the maximum number of challenges allowed to defense counsel), and the state challenged ten. Fifteen were excused on personal grounds—deafness, doctor's orders, and so forth. Twelve jurors and two alternates finally took their seats in the courtroom.

Three hundred and seventy of the prospective jurors—almost 90 per cent—admitted holding some kind of opinion concerning Irvin's guilt. Only a few "suspected" that he was guilty. Many were "certain." Ten of these people were never even asked if they had formed an opinion (Irvin's counsel had used up all his peremptory challenges).

At one point counsel asked the prospective jurors, "If you were on trial for murder and Irvin were a prospective juror who felt as you do about him, would you want him on your jury?" They admitted that they would not.

Of the twelve jurors finally selected, eight quite frankly stated that they believed that Irvin was guilty, but that they would render their final verdict solely on the basis of the evidence admitted in court. One juror even said that he "could not . . . give the defendant the benefit of the doubt that he is innocent."

Irvin was convicted of murder.

The Supreme Court reversed the conviction and ordered a new trial. It held that another change of venue should have been granted. By this reversal the court again pointed out that the brain is, in cases of pre-trial publicity, too efficient an instrument.

As if the problem of pre-trial reporting of facts and confessions isn't difficult enough on its own, a California case illustrates what can happen to jurors when a judge adds his point of view to the newspaper stories.

The case was *People v. McKay*. James McKay and Roger Sturm escaped from a California Youth Authority camp.

After their recapture, while they were being driven back to the camp, they attacked and killed the two men who had captured them—a deputy sheriff and an undersheriff.

These two law officers had been well known and well liked in their community. Outraged by the double murders, the local press played the stories big, and reported that McKay and Sturm had confessed to the slayings.

California authorities were unable to find local counsel who could, conscientiously, defend the accused pair, so the local judge, Judge Ross, appointed counsel from another county. After the appointment, Ross wrote to the local board of supervisors recommending that the new attorneys be reimbursed for their travel expenses.

Then, in a strange twist, the new counsel moved to disqualify Judge Ross because of "prejudice." Their motion carried and Judge Ross was disqualified.

At that point the judge wrote another letter to the board of supervisors. This time he told them that he had reconsidered his original request that the defense attorneys be paid for their travel expenses. He said that they had moved to replace him not because he was partial but because they wanted to postpone the trial as long as possible, thereby causing the county to incur heavy additional expenses—including $5 per day for each of the 125 prospective jurors on the panel of veniremen.

In this letter the judge wrote, ". . . that all four attorneys had stated in our conferences in my office many times that they had gone over the case with the defendants and that *there was no question of the guilt of both defendants of the crime of murder* and that their only hope was to get them off with life imprisonment, although they might try to argue to a jury that it was only second degree murder." (italics added) The letter was printed by the local newspapers.

This was not an unimportant development. Judge Ross was well known and highly respected in the community. The people of the area placed great faith in him. He had been the only regular superior court judge in the county for seventeen years. In his most recent campaign for re-election to the judgeship he had won more votes than any other county officer. Obviously, his point of view would have a great effect on readers.

It did. One juror, under examination by counsel, testified:

Q. You say you did read the judge's letter?
A. Yes.
Q. Was there anything in that letter that would cause you to form an opinion one way or the other concerning the guilt or innocence of the defendants?
A. No. I figure—well, I don't know just how to answer that. As far as making up an opinion. Judge Ross made quite a statement as far as that goes. . . .
Q. Would you say from the recollection of the letter Judge Ross wrote that the judge expressed himself concerning the guilt or innocence of the defendants?
A. Well, I would say he expressed himself, yes.

The defense counsel moved for a change of venue. It was denied. The defendants were convicted of murder.

The Supreme Court of California reversed the conviction. It held that the change of venue should have been granted. Pre-trial publicity, this time abetted by a judge, had again poisoned the minds of prospective jurors.

A remark made earlier in this chapter to the effect that being a woman does not qualify one to be a good mother is illustrated rather gruesomely by another California case. The same case is, too, one more example of the inability of jurors to set aside previously learned facts.

Elizabeth Ann Duncan was the mother. With her son, Frank, she moved to California in 1956. She was a possessive mother, ever fearful that her son, then twenty-seven, would desert her by falling in love and marrying.

At one point, for whatever reason, she took an overdose of sleeping pills. The dose was heavy and dangerous enough to send her to the hospital to recover. Of course, her son visited her at every opportunity.

During one of his visits he met a nurse, Olga. An immediate friendship sprang up and it was apparent to Mrs. Duncan that the relationship was developing into a romantic attachment. She voiced her objections to her son. When that had no effect she threatened Olga, in the presence of a witness, "You'll never marry my son; I'll kill you first."

Frank and Olga were secretly married anyway, in June, 1958. In the middle of July, Mrs. Duncan, more than insanely jealous, hired an ex-convict to pose as Frank while she posed as Olga. Together they went to a judge to try to get an annulment of Frank and Olga's marriage. Each testified that neither was living with the other.

A month or two later Mrs. Duncan hired two men, named Moya and Baldonado, to kill Olga. They agreed on a price of $6,000; $3,000 to be paid before the killing and the other $3,000 afterwards.

In November the two men drove to Olga's apartment. Moya knocked on the door and, when Olga answered, told her that Frank was in the car, drunk, and asking for her help. She went to the car and opened the rear door; on the seat Baldonado was slumped over, pretending to be Frank.

Moya slammed her on the back of the head with a pistol, Baldonado pulled her into the back seat, and they drove off. When Olga showed signs of regaining consciousness Moya struck her with the pistol again, this time so hard that he broke the handle and damaged the firing mechanism.

The original plan had been to drive to Tijuana, in Mexico, and to kill Olga there. However, their car developed some trouble before it reached the border. They pulled over to the side of the road, dragged Olga from the car, and tried to shoot her. The gun was damaged too badly; it would not fire. So the two men took turns strangling her. When they were no longer able to feel her pulse, they buried her near the road.

When the men were caught they quickly implicated Mrs. Duncan, who denied any part in the killing. She was arrested nonetheless. She was also found, by the authorities, to be legally sane.

The murder plan, and the reason behind it, were so bloodthirsty, so animalistic, that the case received almost as much newspaper coverage on the east coast as it did in California. And that was plenty.

While the grand jury investigating the murder was still in session a newspaper article quoted the district attorney as saying, "The brutal, calculated, revolting killing for hire of Olga Duncan is one of a number of horrible crimes which have recently been committed in California. . . . I simply cannot understand how some of our leaders, in the face of these events, can seriously contend that the death penalty is not appropriate for the perpetrators of such a crime."

Even worse, much of the grand jury testimony was published in daily installments in the press. Public officials, including the district attorney, continued to make statements to the press while the case was still under investigation by the grand jury.

The publicity was so intense, so pervasive that, as in the Irvin case in Indiana, it became next to impossible to find jurors who had not formed opinions about Mrs. Duncan's guilt or innocence. Four of the jurors who sat on the jury and later voted to inflict the death penalty on Mrs. Duncan admitted that they were convinced before the trial began that Mrs. Duncan was guilty. They admitted, too, that they would go into the trial knowing that they would require evidence to prove to them that Mrs. Duncan was innocent, rather than evidence to prove her guilty.

They added that they would not want anyone they loved to undergo a trial before jurors who felt as they did, that they were sure such a loved one would not receive a fair trial. ("Would you want a loved one to be tried with you sitting on the jury?" is rather a standard question on the part of defense counsel in trials of this nature.)

Despite all their admissions, they maintained that they could disregard their own opinions; that they would base their verdict on the evidence presented at the trial.

Elizabeth Duncan was tried, convicted, and sentenced to death. The California Supreme Court upheld the conviction. The United States Supreme Court refused to review the case.

One of the great imponderables, always, is the reaction of a court of appeals. There is no way to predict with accuracy whether it will affirm or reverse a conviction. Precedents that seem to apply suddenly do not apply. Other precedents are suddenly overturned in thoroughly unforeseen fashion. (Of course if this were not the case in trials there would be no need for lawyers or judges. If all these matters could be settled predictably, computers could do the job lawyers and judges now do.)

That is precisely why the impact of newspaper and broadcast crime reports on the minds of prospective jurors is so dangerous. There is no certain protection of the courts, even if prejudicial pre-trial publicity is demonstrated. If there were, perhaps we could allow even the irresponsible press to continue its sensationalistic ways. But, given the inconsistency of appeals-court decisions, the task is to provide no information for the spongy brains of potential jurors to absorb, to remember, and to use against a defendant.

In summation one might point to one paragraph of the summation of New Jersey's prosecutor in the case against Bruno Richard Hauptmann in the Lindbergh kidnaping. It was somewhat gobbledygookian, but it leaves no doubt that he was aware of the force of the press on the minds of its readers:

I am not concerned about what the mob is clamoring for. . . but you can bet your life that there is a clamor from the people of this country for this man's conviction. I have sufficient faith in the American people to know that it is their honest belief and conviction that he is a murderer. Otherwise, there would be no clamor, if there is one.

TWO

The Editor as Judge

IT IS PERHAPS too easy to condemn reporters who write
crime stories. They work under the pressure of competition, deadlines, and constant exposure to criminals. They
haven't time to check out every fact, search for exactly the
right word, or examine their finished material for unintended
opinion. Nor, as we will see, do they have any control over
the rewrite man who can make their stories unrecogniz-
able.

But reporters and rewrite men have editors. Ultimately, the
editor is responsible for what appears in his newspaper. He
has the power to kill any story, delete any fact, or change any
word. He, too, might try to claim "too much work, too little
time." But an editor not willing to accept responsibility for
the contents of his paper is neither good for his newspaper nor
good for his profession.

The power of the editor was well illustrated in the closing
days of the presidential campaign of 1964. Less than two
weeks before the election Walter Jenkins, one of President
Johnson's ablest, most trusted assistants, was arrested on a
morals charge. Jenkins was as close to the President as any

aide can be. More than that, he was privy to top-secret information. His arrest on that charge could have swung the election to the Republicans, scandal being always more persuasive than reason in any appeal to the electorate (as crime stories are more salable than texts of speeches to newspaper readers).

President Johnson was in New York when Jenkins was arrested in Washington. The White House staff heard of it before Johnson did. So did two of Johnson's closest nongovernmental advisers, Clark Clifford and Abe Fortas (now Supreme Court Justice Fortas).

Clifford and Fortas, both attorneys, went to the editors of the Washington newspapers and wondered aloud, to those editors, if the Jenkins story should appear "before all the facts were known." The implication of their request, it would seem, was, "Must you run the story?" Apparently the editors understood, for in early editions the story did not appear. However, United Press International broke the news. After that no editor could have been expected to keep the story out of his own pages.

The point is that the editors had the power to broadcast or to withhold the news. The use editors make of this power in reporting crime news is the heart of the problem of trial by newspaper. They can impose tight restrictions, can forbid publication of all but the bare facts. They can refuse to use stories leaked to them, to report confessions before those confessions are admitted into evidence, and to allow reporters to refer to past criminal records. Or they can tolerate all these things—even urge them. They can go further. They can have their newspaper espouse a point of view—in editorial columns, in cartoons, in the wording of headlines or in the elimination of favorable comment.

If an editor's policy is to be sensational, his headline might read: BEAST HUNTED IN ROBBERY AND RAPE OF WIDOW, 71. As indeed a headline read in the New York *Daily News* of September 19, 1962. To a responsible editor, "man" is a much more accurate noun than "beast."

The editor of the New York *World-Telegram & Sun*, on August 3, 1959, allowed his newspaper to describe a defendant's "sneering defiance," after "admitting nothing." That defendant was subsequently acquitted of all charges.

What editors will tolerate is amply illustrated by the following account.

One winter evening two men drove into a gas station in New Britain, Connecticut. While the proprietor was servicing the car one of the men walked into the station "to go to the toilet." The other man paid for the gas, then at gun point forced the proprietor into the boiler room of the station, shot and killed him and took his wallet while the first man was rifling the cash register. They were still inside when another car drove up for gas. They waited for it to drive away, but when it didn't one of the men went out and pretended to service the car. He took out a gun, forced the driver to give up his wallet, then shot him twice in the head while his eighteen-month-old daughter sat alongside.

Two months later, in February, 1957, Culombe and Taborsky were arrested. Newspapers immediately referred to them as the "mad killers." The Hartford *Times* reported Taborsky's earlier criminal record, and reminded readers that he had been released from prison only four years earlier after serving a sentence for a murder conviction. On three successive days that month, before a jury was selected to sit in judgment on the man, the Hartford *Times* repeated that Taborsky, although released from prison, had never been "exonerated."

It also quoted a police official: "Taborsky's story doesn't hold water."

One blaring headline said: CULOMBE IN 8 CONFESSIONS SAYS TABORSKY WAS "MAD KILLER IN STATE'S CRIME WAVE."

The United States Supreme Court subsequently found that Culombe's confessions had been coerced.

The Connecticut editors who allowed these stories to get into print might very well have used the "public good" as their excuse for printing such stories. Many editors like to say that it provides peace of mind to the public to know that killers have been caught.

Connecticut, of course, is on the east coast. But the problem of messianic editors is transcontinental. In California a man named Fouquette, an outpatient at a California insane asylum, was charged with murdering two men. He had been committed to the institution a year earlier, after a court determined that he was legally insane. He had, apparently, recovered sufficiently to become an outpatient.

After Fouquette was charged with the murders, the editor of a local newspaper requested an interview with the district attorney. His request was granted—the following story was the result:

He [the district attorney] believed Fouquette to be absolutely sane before, during, and after the murders . . . "On behalf of law-abiding American citizenry, I am extremely anxious that Fouquette not be found mentally incompetent, so that he may again be paroled, run amok, and claim the lives of other innocent men and wreck the lives of families."

The story then detailed the care with which the district attorney had drafted the confession, in order to make an insanity defense as difficult as possible for the defense to maintain:

Jones [the district attorney], in framing the second written confession, was extremely careful to combat in advance any attempts which might be made at the trial to introduce psychiatric testimony that Fouquette was insane.

One paragraph of the confession, signed by the *killer* [emphasis added] was:

"On August 19, 1948 [the night the victim was brutally slain], at the time I committed the above-mentioned robbery, kidnaping and shooting, I was in my right mind. I knew what I was doing and was not suffering from any influence of any drugs, narcotics, lack of memory, amnesia, or any other mental or physical disability, except that I had been drinking liquor to some extent over a period of several days. I was to some extent under the influence of liquor, but other than that, I had full possession of my faculties. I knew what I was doing and can remember most of the details."

The newspaper also printed the full text of the confession. That kind of zealousness wins Olympic medals for athletes, high grades for scholars, huge commissions for salesmen, and large circulation figures for editors. What it does to a defendant apparently doesn't matter. The editor printed the entire story quoted above before Fouquette was brought to trial.

A man cannot have a fair trial if the public (and his jury) is against him from the start. A determined editor can turn the public against a man. John D. Pennekamp, then associate editor of the Miami *Herald*, did more than just allow the reporting of confessions and leaks. He used his newspaper as a weapon. Mr. Pennekamp ran the following editorial in the Miami *Herald* (1944):

Courts are established for the People. . . .

It is beyond question that American courts are of, by and for the people. Every accused person has a right to his day in court. But when judicial instance and interpretive procedures recognize and accept, even go out to find every possible technicality of the law to protect the defendant, to block, thwart, hinder, embarrass and nullify prosecution, then the people's rights are jeopardized and the basic reason for courts stultified.

The seeming ease and pat facility with which the criminally charged have been given technical safeguards have set people to wondering whether their courts are being subverted into refuges for lawbreakers. This week the people, through their grand jury, brought into court eight indictments for rape. Judge Paul D. Barnes agreed with the defense that the indictments were not properly drawn. Back they went to the grand jury for re-presentation to the court. . . .

With the editorial, Mr. Pennekamp ran a cartoon. The cartoon showed a judge, on the bench, handing a document labeled "defendant dismissed" to an obviously criminal type sitting in the witness chair. The judge was smiling as he did it, and ignoring a puny little figure on his right, labeled "Public Interest," who was pulling at the sleeves of his robe and saying wistfully, "But Judge . . ."

The indictments had been declared invalid because they failed to mention the names of the rape victims. The grand jury that had handed them up was still in session. The indictments went right back to it, new indictments were returned almost immediately, and the defendants were reindicted. All this happened *before* the editorial and the cartoon appeared. Pennekamp knew this or, as a newsman, he should have. He knew that the act he felt was so wrong had been righted, yet he published his editorial and his cartoon nonetheless.

The real danger was his attack on a legal safeguard. There are many and good reasons for these safeguards, all of them having to do with the protection of innocent persons from unjust arrest and imprisonment. Pennekamp, nevertheless, attacked the law as a technicality used to outwit and thwart justice. He wasn't concerned that the same technicality had at other times kept innocent men from wearing a guilty label.

These technicalities that Pennekamp hated crop up in contracts all the time—little fine-print clauses that seem niggling and quibbling. They are inserted to protect one party or the other. It is possible that Pennekamp himself had a contract with his employers. But he chose to deplore legal fine print when it protected a defendant.

Because of the publication of the editorial and cartoon, Pennekamp and the Miami Herald Publishing Company were held in contempt of court. They appealed the contempt citation to the Supreme Court of Florida. The citation was affirmed. Pennekamp was fined $250, the publishing company $1,000.

This decision was appealed to the Supreme Court of the United States. The Supreme Court reversed the lower court's decision. It found that the editorial and the cartoon had not been a clear and present danger to the administration of justice; that to find it so would have been a limitation of the newspaper's freedom of speech. Obviously, it is not safe to assume that the contempt citation is an effective safeguard against the depredations of the press. It is rarely granted and even more rarely affirmed.

Thus we are returned to the root argument of this book— freedoms in collision. In a similar case, the Spokane (Washington) *Press* was also cited for contempt. Its editor, Loren D. Angevine, wrote this editorial, describing an incident in a Spokane courtroom:

ROTTEN

Alone in a man-filled courtroom, Gladys Moore was put through a disgusting rigmarole, by tittering and smirking attorneys in Judge Blake's Court, Friday afternoon.

The girl had charged James Ballmaine with having assaulted her. Prosecutor Jack White and Attorney Bill Donovan took turns at questioning her—questions of the most personal nature.

It was rich stuff for the onlookers, among whom were boys of tender years.

Donovan and White took it lightly, for they smiled and winked at friends in the crowd.

The *Press* knows nothing about Gladys Moore; but the *Press* knows that such a thing as this shouldn't be aired in open court. Common decency should have prompted Judge Blake to call the case in chambers and to have reprimanded the attorneys for their failure to realize that the thing was deadly serious.

The editorial, coming as it did while the trial was still in session, might easily have provoked great sympathy for Miss Moore, even greater antagonism toward Mr. Ballmaine, who had been accused of assaulting her.

Editor Angevine was cited for contempt of court. The grand jury handed up an indictment supporting the contempt citation. In the indictment, the grand jury pointed out that the editorial was inaccurate and in parts untrue. Gladys Moore was not the only woman in the courtroom (the editorial had made it seem she was by the phrase "man-filled courtroom"). Prosecutor White did not take turns questioning Miss Moore—he didn't even participate in the trial. And the judge could not have tried the case in his chambers; the law requires that trials be held in open court.

The foregoing took place in 1919. Since then, our Supreme Court has tended to uphold the primacy of freedom of speech. Only recently has there been a renewed outcry against trial by newspaper. Perhaps the following cases contributed to the present awareness of the problem.

Judge Joe D. Browning, presiding in the County Court of
Nueces County, Texas, was sitting in a case involving a landlord who was suing a tenant for nonpayment of rent due on a
bar and grill. The tenant, a veteran of World War II, had
admittedly failed to pay his rent. But this was shortly after the
war when veterans were still heroes, particularly in small
towns. There was, however, no doubt that the landlord was
justified in trying to reclaim his property.

Accordingly (as was his right), Judge Browning directed
the jury to return a verdict in the landlord's favor. The jury
refused, and found in favor of the tenant. The judge explained that he was bound to refuse that verdict and again
asked the jury for a verdict in favor of the landlord. Again the
jury refused; and a third time, too. At that point the tenant's
lawyer, sorrowfully, advised the jury that it stood in danger of
contempt if it did not follow the judge's direction. Only then
did it return a decision for the landlord.

The tenant's lawyer asked for a new trial and Judge
Browning took the matter under advisement. Three days later
the Corpus Christi (Texas) papers, the *Caller* and the *Times*
(both under the same ownership), published the following
editorial:

Browning's behavior and attitude has brought down the
wrath of public opinion upon his head, properly so. Emotions
have been aggravated. American people simply don't like the
idea of such goings on, especially when a man in the service
of his country seems to be getting a raw deal. . . .

That was a travesty on justice. . . . That's where a legal
background would have served him in good stead [Judge
Browning, who had been elected to the bench, did not have a
law degree]. It is difficult to believe that any lawyer, even a
hack, would have followed such high-handed procedure in
instructing a jury. It is no wonder that the jury balked and
public opinion outraged. . . .

The editorial appeared while Judge Browning was still considering the motion for a new trial. He denied the motion. Then he cited the publisher of the newspapers, their managing editor, and a reporter, for contempt in attempting to influence the decision of a pending case. He sentenced them to three days in jail each.

Who can tell if the judge refused the new trial as a show of strength against the editorial, or on the merits of the case? What if he had been intimidated by the editorial, and had ordered a new trial out of fear of press criticism?

The Texas Court of Criminal Appeals affirmed the contempt citation. That affirmation was in turn appealed to the United States Supreme Court, but before we consider the decision of the Supreme Court in that case, there is another case to review—involving three counts of contempt against the Los Angeles *Times*.

In its coverage of three different trials, the Los Angeles paper made less than impartial statements about the defendants. The first trial involved several sit-down strikers (the strike was against the Douglas Aircraft Company) on trial in Los Angeles for damaging buildings and equipment of Douglas. They were found guilty. Before they were sentenced, the Los Angeles *Times* said editorially:

The verdict means Los Angeles is still Los Angeles, that the city is aroused to the danger of davebeckism, and that no kind of union terrorism will be permitted here. . . .

. . . It is an important verdict. For the first time since the present cycle of labor disturbances began, union lawlessness has been treated as exactly what it is, an offense against the public peace punishable like any other crime. . . .

So long as that is the case, davebeckism cannot and will not get control here, nor johnlewisism either.

A year later Mrs. Helen M. Werner, a political power in

Los Angeles, was indicted for attempting to bribe a deputy district attorney. She was convicted. While a motion for a new trial was pending, and again *before* the judge pronounced sentence on her, the Los Angeles *Times* had some editorial comments to make:

THE FALL OF AN EX-QUEEN

Mrs. Werner's primary mistake seems to have been in failing to recognize that her political day was past. For years she enjoyed the unique distinction of being the country's only woman boss—and did she enjoy it! In her heyday, she had a finger in every political pie and many were the plums she was able to extract therefrom. . . . She became a power in the backstage councils of city and county affairs and from that place of strategic advantage reached out to pull the strings on state and legislative offices as well. . . .

Those were the days when Mrs. Werner was "Queen Helen". . . .

A month later, in the same year, Matthew Shannon and Kennan Holmes were tried and found guilty of assault. They were former employees of the May Company of Los Angeles. The assault they were convicted of was committed during a strike of delivery and warehouse employees against the May Company. This is what the Los Angeles *Times* had to say:

PROBATION FOR GORILLAS?

Two members of Dave Beck's wrecking crew, entertainment committee, goon squad or gorillas, having been convicted in Superior Court of assaulting nonunion truck drivers, have asked for probation. Presumably they will say they are "first offenders," or plead that they were merely indulging in playful exuberance when, with slingshots, they fired steel missiles at men whose only offense was wishing to work for a living without paying tribute to the erstwhile boss of Seattle. . . .

It will teach no lesson to other thugs to put these men on good behavior for a limited time. Their "duty" would simply be taken over by others like them. If Beck's thugs, however, are made to realize that they face San Quentin when they are caught, it will tend to make their disreputable occupation unpopular. *Judge A. A. Scott will make a serious mistake if he grants probation to Matthew Shannon and Kennan Holmes. This community needs the example of their assignment to the Jute Mill.* [italics added]

This time the newspaper's editors not only editorialized before sentencing, they mentioned the judge by name and urged explicitly that he impose harsh sentences.

Finally, it was all too much for the Los Angeles Bar Association. It sought and won a contempt citation against the *Times* for its editorial treatment of the three cases. For its efforts, the bar association was crucified by the entire Los Angeles press. It was accused of trying to "nazify the courts," and to "create star-chamber sessions."

However, the California Supreme Court upheld each of the contempt counts and had this to say in the instance of the Douglas Aircraft strikers:

The editorial may not have been intended, but it is capable of being construed, as a notice to the trial judge that no leniency should be extended to the convicted men, and, furthermore, that should the court act contrary to the suggestions contained in the editorial, it might expect adverse criticism in the columns of the *Times.*

In the matter of Mrs. Werner, the court felt that the editorial could have exercised a covert influence on the judge. He had not yet sentenced her or decided on her motion for a new trial. If he had been lenient, or granted the new trial, it could have been interpreted by the public, in the light of the editorial, as bowing to any remaining influence Mrs. Werner might still have had.

The Los Angeles *Times* appealed the decision to the U.S. Supreme Court.

The Supreme Court reversed all the citations. It decided that the citations impinged upon the *Times'* freedom of speech. It made the same determination in the Corpus Christi, Texas, case. The court found no clear and present danger, and concluded that the contempt citation unfairly limited the *Caller's* and the *Times'* freedom of speech.

The United States Supreme Court is under attack today from southern legislators for its decisions in civil-rights cases. These southerners (and some northern legal experts, too) maintain that the court has gone too liberal, that it is not interpreting the Constitution but writing it. The majority of legal opinion in the country, however, feels that the court is acting absolutely within the powers given it by the Constitution. At the same time, one cannot deny that today's court is far different in philosophy from any court prior to it.

Today's court has made decision after decision respecting and upholding the rights of the individual. In 1963, its landmark *Gideon v. Wainwright* decision for the first time guaranteed the right to counsel of even the most impoverished defendant in the smallest state court. Gideon was impoverished. He was also an alcoholic, a drifter, and a man with a long criminal record. After his arrest, the Florida court where he was tried refused his request for counsel. Gideon was convicted. He appealed his conviction to the U.S. Supreme Court and the court stood by him. He was an individual and an American and, as such, he was entitled to the rights granted him by his Constitution.

It is not farfetched to believe that the U.S. Supreme Court

will one day be called upon, again, to decide a case of trial by newspaper, or of a newspaper editor's attempt to influence justice through use of his editorial columns. What will the decision be?

Felix R. McKnight is vice-president and editor of the Dallas *Times Herald.* He is also a former Nieman Fellow, one of the highest honors in journalism. In August, 1964, Mr. McKnight, a former president of the American Society of Newspaper Editors, addressed the American Bar Association at its convention in New York City. He talked about trial by newspaper.

I suggest that we are confronted with the problem of human frailties [all italics author's]—not the degeneration of the free press or the occasional failures of the bar and bench. Old-fashioned as it might sound, we are dealing with the integrity, the principles and the judgment of individuals.

No happening should give greater test to editorial skill than the violent death of a President. . . .

Yet, *when the greatest degree of fidelity to purpose was demanded, some of the American press faltered.* In waves of hundreds they came to our city—men, microphones, and camera. Three hundred of them came to cover the death of a President and the indefensible loss of his accused assassin. *And then 371, to report in varying degrees of accuracy, the trial of strip-tease-joint operator Jack Ruby.* . . .

We were indeed an uninspiring sight on national television at the conclusion of the Jack Ruby trial in Dallas. Newspapers, radio and television reporters shouting inane questions in the courtroom; clambering over courtroom furniture, fighting for positions; shoving countless microphones into the face of that courtroom exhibitionist, Melvin Belli. . . .

Editor Benjamin McKelway of the Washington Star *states clearly the position of the American press when he emphasizes that what is published may at times obscure or even destroy a presumption of innocence by the public at large—if not the jurors sitting on a law case—concerning someone under accusation of wrongdoing.*

But, the source of such prejudicial information in the press may be a privileged congressional investigation. It may be an utterance by a President of the United States, accompanied by finger shaking and the elaborate window dressing of a televised press conference. It may be the indictment of an individual which sets in motion a tidal wave of speculation as to how many others may be involved . . . before anybody has been tried or found guilty of anything.

The source of such prejudicial information may be a statement by an Attorney-General or other Cabinet officer or member of Congress. It may be a calculated leak to the press, sometimes from highly authoritative and responsible officers of the court, of information not yet proved or even admitted as evidence in court but definitely prejudicial to the rights of an accused if he ever gets into court. . . .

Of course there are available illustrations of that condition known as "trial by newspaper" in which newspapers have employed every device of inflammatory sensationalism, rationalizing their unfairness and their defiance of others' rights by proclaiming the people's right to know while reaping the benefits of increased circulation in serving that right. . . .

That, of course, is irresponsible journalism. . . .

Irresponsible journalism might be consigned to a category that also includes incompetent, corrupt, or politically motivated judges and unethical lawyers who also contribute to erosion of justice. . . .

In our ranks are many editors of many stripes. Most, I would venture, oppose the thought of codes, legal restrictions backed by sanctions or any other harnessing device. We prefer to exercise our own sense of responsibility. . . .

Faith is sometimes a slender reed. But faith in continuing development of the responsibility that *must* accompany freedom of the press, and faith in the progress of our whole society toward a more sophisticated civilization, is a better reed to lean on than a return by the courts to use of summary contempt in punishing newspapers. . . .

To work backward through Mr. McKnight's speech, the only thing in this world we are asked to accept on faith is the existence of God, and there are apparently fewer and fewer people willing to do that. In fact, it is generally recognized as not only good business but sound legal practice to have written agreements or signed leases and written guarantees rather than to do business on a matter-of-faith basis. No one in business in this country proceeds on faith; indeed it is considered unsound practice by the best business schools in the land. Why, then, does Mr. McKnight advocate a rule of faith in the realm of journalism? He himself admits that journalism is a business, a business for profit which comes through circulation.

He says that "irresponsible journalism" should be lumped with irresponsible, corrupt, unethical lawyers and judges. Does he not realize that there are legal sanctions to deal with the corrupt? Has his newspaper never reported that a judge or a lawyer has gone to jail for unethical or corrupt practices? To lump newspapers with judges and lawyers would be to apply legal sanctions against newspapers for misuses of their freedom, a possibility Mr. McKnight contemplates with horror.

Mr. McKnight blames the leaker. He does not say that a leak is meaningless and powerless unless it appears in print or on the air. Yet that is the case. No one forces his newspaper, or any other, to print leaks. A party to a crime, in criminal law, can be named an "accessory after the fact" even though he had nothing to do with the commission of that crime. If a newspaper prints a prejudicial leak, is it not an accessory? Some newspaper editors draw strange distinctions.

He asserts that only a few journalists descend to shameful levels. Yet he points out that the Dallas courtroom where Jack Ruby was convicted was carnage itself, with fighting, pushing, and screamed questions going out over the air waves to the entire nation.

And he says, "I suggest that we are confronted with the problem of human frailties—not the degeneration of the free press."

Every criminal law statute we have in our land, possibly in the entire world, was written because of a human frailty— real or anticipated. If the press is that humanly frail, it, too, must submit to laws.

Mr. McKnight spoke as vice-president and editor of one of the major newspapers of the country. He spoke, too, as a former elected president of the American Society of Newspaper Editors. Since an election generally represents majority opinion, it can be assumed that Mr. McKnight's attitudes coincide with those of most other newspaper editors. If that is the case, the battle for a more responsible press will be a difficult one.

There is no more perfect example of the dereliction of our nation's editors than occurred in the case of Dr. Sam Sheppard, in Cleveland, Ohio. Almost every editor in the country, certainly every editor of a major newspaper, was responsible for the kind of coverage given to the murder trial of Dr. Sheppard. The reporters and columnists at that trial represented not only the "irresponsible few" referred to by Mr. McKnight. They represented the national press. They were sent there, by the dozens, by their editors.

Before the case was one week old, people all over the country were saying, "Sheppard did it himself." This reaction was based solely on information disseminated by newspapers, radio, and television. There was no other way to get the information.

The coverage was fierce and biased. Columnists posed questions to themselves, the answers unstated but pointing toward the guilt of "Dr. Sam." *Time* reported that Dr. Sheppard had been called "the Romeo of the rubbing table." The press had a field day. A graphic example of what we are discussing is the activities of the Cleveland *Press*, part of the Scripps-Howard chain. Its editor, Louis B. Seltzer, was acclaimed then and still is acclaimed one of the finest editors in the country. If his performance was the act of a fine newspaper editor, there is no doubt that legislation is needed to protect citizens from their newspapers. The behavior of the editor of the Cleveland *Press* is eminent justification of the need for it. (The other Cleveland newspapers acted somewhat more responsibly—but only by comparison.)

The murder, committed on July 4, 1954, immediately attracted nationwide attention. Sheppard was a prosperous osteopathic physician, son of a noted family, a member of the "right" Cleveland society. He had an attractive wife and a five-year-old son. The ingredients were right for the newspapers.

Early in the morning of July 4, Sam Sheppard called the mayor of Bay Village, his little community outside Cleveland, to mumble a dazed story about a "bushy-haired man" who invaded his home, killed his wife with a blunt instrument, knocked him out when he tried to catch him, and escaped. Dr. Sheppard's son, Chip, slept through the attack.

There were no clues to point to an unknown suspect. No fingerprints, no strange footprints, no trace of the weapon. Suspicion immediately centered on Dr. Sheppard himself.

Twelve days after the murder no arrests had been made. On July 16, 1954, editor Seltzer's number-one editorial read:

THE FINGER OF SUSPICION

The worst thing about the tragic mishandling of the Sheppard murder investigation is the resulting suspicion.

Why was it mishandled, people ask?

You can't blame them . . .

What happened, then?

Two things stood in the way of the usual complete and unfettered investigation that citizens of Greater Cleveland have come to expect. . . .

One was the hostility of Bay Village officials to any "outsiders" in this case. They rebuffed the usual assistance immediately offered by Cleveland police experts in solving murders.

Second was the unusual protection set up around the husband of the victim, [all italics added by author] the sole witness, according to later reports, who could start the investigation on the right track.

The protection was twofold. It came from his family and it came from his lawyer. It was unusual, to say the least . . .

It was bad for everybody. Everybody, that is, except the murderer.

What can be done, now? . . .

First logical step would be a meeting of all the law enforcement agencies involved. Let them select a leader . . .

Let him serve notice that protection, special favors and fancy ultimatums by lawyers are out from here on. . . .

There could have been little doubt, after reading that editorial, about the identity of the prime suspect as far as the Cleveland *Press* was concerned.

Four days later, on July 20, the *Press* went at it again. This time its editorial made the first one look like a model of impartiality. On the front page, straight across the top of the page—the spot usually reserved for declarations of war—was this editorial:

SHEPHARD SET FOR NEW QUIZ

Getting Away with Murder

An Editorial

What's the matter with the law enforcement authorities of Cuyahoga County? . . .

In the background of this case are friendships, relationships, hired lawyers, a husband who ought to have been subjected instantly to the same third-degree [author's italics here and below] to which any other person under similar circumstances is subjected, and a whole string of special and bewildering extra-privileged courtesies that should never be extended by authorities investigating a murder—the most serious, and sickening crime of all.

The spectacle of a whole community watching a batch of law enforcement officials fumbling around, stumbling over one another, bowing and scraping in the presence of people they ought to be dealing with as firmly as any other persons in any other crime—that spectacle is not only becoming a stench but a serious threat to the dignity of law enforcement itself.

Coroner Sam Gerber was never more right than when yesterday he said that the killer must be laughing secretly at the whole spectacle—the spectacle of a community of a million and a half people brought to indignant frustration by Mrs. Sheppard's killer in that white house out in Bay Village.

Why shouldn't he chuckle? Why shouldn't he cover up, shut up, conceal himself behind the circle of protecting people? . . .

It's time that somebody smashed into this situation and tore aside this restraining curtain of sham, politeness and hypocrisy and went at the business of solving a murder—and quit this nonsense of artificial politeness that has not been extended to any other murder case in generations.

On July 21, the Cleveland *News*, which bills itself "A

Friend of the Family," joined in the chorus. In an editorial it stated:

TIME TO BRING BAY
SLAYING INTO OPEN

Too many days have passed without positive results in the several investigations of the Bay Village hack-slaying. . . .

We are forced to take note that Dr. Samuel Sheppard, husband of the victim has rejected suggestions of both lie detector and truth serum tests, and his submitting to questioning only when his family and his lawyer have agreed he might. . . .

The *News* did not point out that there are many authorities who have no faith at all in the accuracy of either the lie detector or truth serum; that there are cases on record of lie detectors being totally inaccurate or unreadable.

Nor did it bother to explain that the entire function of a lawyer is to protect his client, to see to it that he gets due process of law. Questioning need not be by police officers in police stations. The function of a grand jury is to determine whether or not the evidence is sufficient to indict. If Dr. Sheppard's lawyer insisted that questioning take place only before a grand jury he was well within his rights, and probably very smart.

The next day, July 22, the *Press* was back in the fray. Another editorial said:

GET THAT KILLER

It is high time that strenuous action be taken in the Sheppard murder case. . . .

True, the case is cold as ice. There has, in our opinion, been a noticeable lack of cooperation on the part of the dead woman's husband, Dr. Samuel M. Sheppard, who has refused to take a lie detector test, and who yesterday rejected proposals that he submit to a "truth serum" test.

He had already been subjected to interrogation, he said; he could not face further interrogation because he is still emotionally upset, and he was reluctant to put himself in a position where he might involuntarily incriminate innocent people.

The last noble sentiment would, we feel, have been far more noble if Dr. Sheppard had said; "I will be happy to do anything within my power to bring my wife's murderer to justice. If a lie dector test would help, by all means bring it on. If a "truth serum" test would convince you that I have told police all I know in an honest effort to apprehend the murderer, I am at your service, gentlemen." . . .

Finding the killer should be of the greatest satisfaction to Greater Cleveland, to Bay Village, and to Dr. Samuel Sheppard. [author's italics]

When had the editor of the Cleveland *Press* last heard of "innocent till proven guilty"?

Finally, on July 28, Louis Seltzer dropped all pretense at subtlety and got down to the business of being his own judge and jury in the Sam Sheppard case. The Cleveland *Press* asked:

WHY DON'T POLICE
QUIZ TOP SUSPECT?

An Editorial

You can bet your last dollar the Sheppard murder would be cleaned up long ago if it had involved "average people."

They'd have hauled in all the suspects to Police Headquarters.

They'd have grilled them in the accepted, straight-out way of doing police business.

They wouldn't have waited so much as one hour to bring the chief suspect in.

Much less days.

Much less weeks.

Why all this fancy, high-level bowing and scraping, and supercautious monkey business? . . .

They'd have Sam Sheppard brought in, grill him at Police Headquarters, like the chief suspect in any murder case. . . . [author's italics here and below]

Now proved under oath to be a liar, still free to go about his business shielded by his family, *protected by a smart lawyer who has made monkeys of the police and authorities,* carrying a gun part of the time, left free to do whatever he pleases, Sam Sheppard still hasn't been taken to headquarters. . . .

It's just about time that somebody began producing the answers— And producing Sam Sheppard at Police Headquarters.

July 29. The *Press* published a cartoon showing a pair of handcuffed hands, labeled "officials" and "police." The hands were reaching out toward, but couldn't reach, a man shielded from sight by a sheet labeled "murder suspect." The sheet was held in front of him by two groups of people marked "lawyers" and "friends." The caption on the cartoon read: "Handcuffs on the Wrong People?"

On July 30, the *Press* ran one editorial twice—changing the headline over it between editions. The first time it ran on page one, across the top of the page again. The headline asked: WHY ISN'T SAM SHEPPARD IN JAIL? In the next edition the headline ordered: QUIT STALLING—BRING HIM IN.

Maybe somebody in this town can remember a parallel for it. The *Press* can't.

And not even the oldest police veterans can, either.

Everybody's agreed that Sam Sheppard is the most unusual murder suspect ever seen around these parts.

Except for some superficial questioning during Coroner Sam Gerber's inquest he has been scot-free of any official grilling into the circumstances of his wife's murder.

From the morning of July 4, when he reported his wife's killing, to this moment, 26 days later, Sam Sheppard has not set foot in a police station.

He has been surrounded by an iron curtain of protection that makes Malenkov's Russian concealment amateurish. [author's italics here and below]

His family, his Bay Village friends—which include its officials—his lawyers, his hospital staff, have combined to make law enforcement in this county look silly.

The longer they can stall bringing Sam Sheppard to the police station the surer it is he'll never get there.

The longer they can string this whole affair out the surer it is that the public's attention sooner or later will be diverted to something else, and then the heat will be off, the public interest gone, and the goose will hang high.

This man is a suspect in his wife's murder. Nobody yet has found a solitary trace of the presence of anybody else in his Lake Rd. house the night or morning his wife was brutally beaten to death in her bedroom.

And yet no murder suspect in the history of this county has been treated so tenderly, with such infinite solicitude for his emotions, with such fear of upsetting the young man.

Gentlemen of Bay Village, Cuyahoga County, and Cleveland, charged jointly with law enforcement. . . .

A murder has been committed. You know who the chief suspect is.

You have the obligation to question him—question him thoroughly and searchingly—from beginning to end, and not at his hospital, not at his home, not in some secluded spot out in the country.

But at Police Headquarters . . .

What . . . the *Press* cannot understand is why you are showing Sam Sheppard so much more consideration as a murder suspect than any other person who has ever before been suspected in a murder case. Why?

If the Cleveland *Press* had been judge and jury, as indeed it tried to be, Sam Sheppard would at that moment have been sitting in a gas chamber, inhaling deeply.

Sam Sheppard was indicted. To this day no one can know how deeply the grand jury was influenced by the campaign against Sheppard waged by the Cleveland *Press*.

In October, 1954, Dr. Sheppard went to trial. The *Press*, page one again, again goes to the attack:

BUT WHO WILL SPEAK FOR MARILYN?

It's perfect, you think at first, as you look over the setting for the Big Trial.

The courtroom is just the size to give a feeling of coziness and to put the actors close enough to each other so that in moments of stress the antagonists can stand jaw to jaw. . . .

Modern enough for this "See-Hear" age, with the microphone, the loudspeaker, and the blazing lights for the TV cameras before and after court sessions. . . .

These provide the perfect background for the most perfect character of all—the accused. Was there ever a more perfect typing? Was there ever a more perfect face for the enigma that is the Big Trial?

Study the face as long as you want. Never will you get from it a hint of what might be the answer when the curtain rings down on this setting and on these characters. Is he the one? Did he do it?

Plus, of course, the other characters. The accused's two brothers. Prosperous, poised. His two sisters-in-law. Smart, chic, well-groomed. His elderly father. Courtly, reserved. A perfect type for the patriarch of a staunch clan. . . .

No, there's something—and someone missing.

The story goes on to talk about Marilyn Sheppard. She is the "something"—"someone" missing. It concludes:

Then you realize how what and who is missing from the perfect setting will be supplied.

How in the Big Case justice will be done.

Justice to Sam Sheppard. [Notice it doesn't say "justice for Sam Sheppard."]

And to Marilyn Sheppard.

In November, with the trial still in progress, the *Press* took to its front page again:

SAM CALLED A "JEKYLL-HYDE"

BY MARILYN, COUSIN TO TESTIFY

Two days before her death, murdered Marilyn Reese Sheppard told friends that her accused husband, Dr. Samuel M. Sheppard, was a "Dr. Jekyll and Mr. Hyde."

The prosecution has a "bombshell witness" on tap who will testify to Dr. Sam's display of fiery temper—countering the defense claim that the defendant is a gentle physician with an even disposition. . . .

Mrs. Sheppard used the "Jekyll-Hyde" expression frequently in confidential conversations during the past several years, friends and relatives have told the murder investigators.

The "bombshell witness" is Thomas Weigle, 26, . . . Marilyn's first cousin. . . .

The story continues by describing what, to the cousin, was a vicious beating administered by Sheppard to his son, Chip. Sheppard's lawyer claims that it was administered because the son threw something at his mother.

That testimony hadn't even been given in court yet. It couldn't have been. It was hearsay and therefore inadmissible. That didn't stop the *Press*.

Sheppard was convicted and sent to jail. One trusts that the Cleveland *Press* was, and remains, proud of the part it played in helping "justice" triumph. That was an example indeed of the press at its most honorable, giving its all because the "public has a right to know." That was an example indeed of an honored editor making our press something to be proud of.

In 1964, ten years later, Dr. Sam Sheppard was released from jail on an appeal by his lawyers that their 1954 motions for a change of venue should have been granted because the press had made it impossible for him to get a fair trial. Either an innocent man spent ten harrowing years in jail—or a guilty murderer went free, because the press refused to exercise its responsibilities.

Editors seem to have a special feeling against anyone named Sheppard. In *Shepard v. Florida* (a completely different Shepard), four Negroes were charged with the rape of a seventeen-year-old white girl. As the grand jury met to hear evidence, the local paper published a cartoon showing simply four electric chairs. The caption? NO COMPROMISE—SUPREME PENALTY. Still we continue to live with the fiction that the editors of the press must be uninhibited by legal restraint.

THREE

The Unpluggable Dike:
Leaks to the Press

POLICEMEN frequently tell the press about a crime they have "solved," overlooking the fact that a crime is not solved until the defendant is found guilty. The press reports the story, maintaining that this is its job.

Sometimes, though, official policy prohibits the release of these stories. Somehow they find their way into the newspapers anyway. They are "leaked" to reporters by "authoritative sources," "reliable sources," and "responsible officials." No one is quoted directly. Readers understand.

The police are seldom reluctant to leak a story to the press, no matter what the consequences to the defendant. (The police are quite upset, though, when the worm turns and outsiders complain to the press of unnecessary police brutality.)

Leaking stories to the press has many benefits, few of them to the defendant. Making the department look good is not the least of these benefits. Moreover, if a case seems weak the unattributed release of details of the crime or confession can inflame the public to the point where a jury drawn from that public is more likely to return a guilty verdict. Nor are the police alone in the use of this ploy. The defense can use the press for its own purposes, and often does. If through astute usage of the public-relations power of the press, the defense can generate sympathy for the defendant, chances for a not-guilty verdict, or a lighter sentence, are multiplied. In each case the press is a willing, knowing accomplice. One does not balance the other, though. The public always seems more willing to believe police and prosecution than the defense, particularly if the crime is sufficiently vicious and bloody.

There are codes of ethics, honored mainly in the breach, to deal with these problems. Lawyers, whether for the prosecution or for the defense, are not supposed to give out information. (A senator known to the author knows what to do with codes of ethics. He took the code passed by the U.S. Senate, framed it, and hung it on the inside of his bathroom door.)

Frequently, when it is unethical to issue such information, attorneys (on both sides) turn to the "leak." These are the only leaks in the world we try to enlarge; there is no finger in *this* dike. Instead, we can detect multitudes of hands, scrabbling, scratching and tearing, trying to enlarge it.

The problem is receiving the attention it deserves, if not the curatives it needs. In 1954, New York District Attorney Frank Hogan, recognized everywhere as one of the fairest district attorneys the country has ever known, imposed on his staff a rule against giving out news of confessions in advance of trial. He had decided that printing the details of a confession was prejudicial to a defendant. The press, apparently, was not as concerned as Frank Hogan. It attacked Mr. Hogan for his decision.

On April 22, 1954, just a few weeks after Mr. Hogan issued his commandment, he felt compelled to defend his position against the attacks by the press. He made his defense in a letter to the New York *Law Journal*. Excerpts from this letter follow:

During the past two months editorials have appeared in several N.Y. City newspapers commenting upon my policy of declining to disclose the contents of statements made by prospective defendants in criminal investigations, or to characterize such statements as confessions. With one exception, these editorials have been extremely critical, their general tenor being that this policy constitutes a press "gag," a news "blackout" or an "iron curtain" of "censorship."

These characterizations are completely misleading. The policy assailed does not cloak criminal cases or investigations with an atmosphere of secrecy. In no wise does it conceal the commission of any crime, the occurrence of any arrest, the identity of any defendant or the nature of any charge. The sole purpose is to protect the right of a defendant to a fair trial by not disclosing, before trial, that he may have incriminated himself.

The salutary purpose of this policy is so obvious and is so uniformly recognized by the judiciary and the legal profession that I am surprised that anyone should question, ignore or discount it. It seems undeniable that widely disseminated information that a defendant has "confessed" has the effect of convincing the general public that he is unquestionably guilty and that any trial will be a mere formality. To obtain an impartial jury under such circumstances, therefore, may be a most difficult task. In its practical effect, such publication tends to destroy the presumption that an accused is innocent until he is proven guilty beyond a reasonable doubt in a court of law.

The vice inherent in the situation stands out in bolder relief where the statement is never even received in evidence. Such a statement sometimes is excluded as not being a confession at all by a court ruling that duress preceded or accompanied it; or that it was given under some inducement or promise of benefit; or that it resulted from some unfair psychological pressure; or that the person was in such an unstable mental condition at the time as to preclude credence of any statement made by him. For these or similar reasons, indeed, the prosecutor himself may decide not to offer the statement in evidence at the trial.

On May 14, 1954, the New York *Times* used its editorial page to compliment Mr. Hogan for his stand. The editorial said:

We must say that we see no workable method to guarantee fair trial that does not impose restraint on officials and lawyers, and that we see no invasion of the basic rights of free press in silence so imposed. If officials talk, if lawyers comment on their cases anticipated or pending, newspapers— even responsible ones—will surely vary in their interpretation of any code of ethics for their own profession. If officials and lawyers don't comment, then there can be no opportunity for violation or variation by the newspapers.

Officials and lawyers have a right and a duty, in the public interest, to impose self-restraints that will protect civil liberties and fair trial. They are thus censoring themselves. The newspapers have an obligation likewise in the public interest to accept the consequences of this act of conscience.

The *Times* passes the buck when it says, "If officials and lawyers don't comment, then there can be no opportunity for violation or variation by the newspapers." Does the *Times* really mean that it cannot control itself, that if a district attorney says what he shouldn't say, the *Times* must publish it? Is that "All the News That's Fit to Print"?

Despite Mr. Hogan's rule, this story appeared in the New York *World-Telegram* on November 17, 1964. It referred to a famous jewel robbery.

In New York, District Attorney Frank S. Hogan's office declined to confirm or deny reports today that Kuhn and Murphy had been named in the sealed indictment. But *another source in the Criminal Courts building* said the two men had been named. [italics added]

Apparently the press prefers the position taken by George B. DeLuca, former district attorney for Bronx County in New York State. At about the same time that Mr. Hogan forbade his assistants to reveal details of confessions, Mr. DeLuca said:

I think it must be conceded at the outset that in recent years there has been a growing tendency on the part of prosecutors, attorneys, the police and perhaps others, to divulge to the press before trial a great deal of the evidence in pending court cases which have news value. . . .

I deduce . . . that there is not the slightest indication, not to say proof, in our county, at least, that prior press coverage has adversely affected the defendant in any given case. I think it is fair to say, it is only in the *cause célèbre*, the kind that arises most infrequently that prior press coverage conceivably might leave an adverse impression upon the mind of a prospective juror which might require evidence to eradicate. While I do not condone or approve the conduct of some sections of the press in their handling of crime or other sensational news, it is my considered opinion that the potential for harm has been grossly exaggerated out of all proportion to actualities.

The Bronx, Mr. DeLuca's (then) domain, is across a tiny river from Manhattan, where Mr. Hogan works. New York City's newspapers cover both territories. Mr. Hogan's point of view is the proper one, but Mr. DeLuca's is the more productive for all but the defendant. And what of the *"cause célèbre*," the "infrequent" cases referred to by Mr. DeLuca? Don't the defendants in those cases matter?

As an example of just how insoluble this problem is without the imposition of legal restraints on the press, consider these remarks of Alexander F. Jones, executive editor of the Syracuse *Herald-Journal*, and past president of the Society of American Newspaper Editors:

What difference does it make, then, in the final analysis, whether a confession is prepublished or produced in evidence? The impact on the defendant would be greater in the latter case. The fate of the defendant would be the same.

What pre-trial publication does is to make the task of the defendant's counsel harder up to the point of acceptance of the confession in evidence. Then his goose is cooked anyway.

As long as there are editors who hold this point of view, and act on it, other editors—though better intentioned—will have to compete with them on their own grounds.

The New York *Journal-American* of August 29, 1956, provides an all-too-perfect example of a newspaper using leaks to build a sensational story. The italics in the following quotation were added to indicate a "leaker" who refused to be quoted directly.

HINT DIO ORDERED DEATH OF TELVI IN RIESEL CASE

A reluctant parade of East Side hoodlums stole [the] spotlight at Federal Court today as FBI brought in men accused of masterminding the acid blinding of Victor Riesel. First to arrive was gang czar Johnny "Dio" Dioguardi . . . accused of engineering the attack.

"Weak Link" Helped FBI

Johnny Dio, one of the nation's top labor racketeers, may have ordered the murder of Abe Telvi when he became a "nuisance" following the acid attack on labor columnist Victor Riesel, *it was learned today.*

This disclosure was made as Dio and four alleged conspirators were arraigned in a heavily guarded court. . . .

Shortly *before* the arraignment at which U.S. Attorney Paul Williams sketched out the case against Dio, the *Journal-American learned* that the FBI cracked the Riesel case and its many ramifications through exerting pressure on a "weak link" in the underworld organization.

The person who informed on Dio and his associates is a ranking member of the outfit, *it was learned,* who cracked under pressure and "squealed" despite his fear of the underworld's death penalty for informing.

The FBI source indicated that the "squealer" was confronted with a choice of two evils—informing on his friends or taking the rap himself.

"He decided to talk," *the Journal-American was told.*

The story appeared on page one, along with a photograph showing Johnny Dio handcuffed. When it appeared, Johnny Dio had not only not been tried, he had not even been indicted by a grand jury. Theoretically, an impartial grand jury could have decided there was insufficient proof of wrongdoing, and refused to indict Dio. He was indicted. But no one can say how many of the grand jurors had read that story and, no matter how involuntarily, been prejudiced by it. It is possible, in fact, that that story was leaked precisely in order to prejudice some of the grand jurors. No one will ever know that, either. Dio was later convicted in court, and sentenced to jail. He could never have been tried if the grand jury had not indicted him.

In 1949, in California, a District Attorney Simpson did not even have the discretion to "leak" his information. He used the "open" leak. To secure a conviction, he ladled information to the press *as* the suspect was making his confession. The

information he gave appeared in the following form in the
Los Angeles *Times* of November 18, 1949:

CONFESSION SCENE STEEPED IN DRAMA
FBI MEN ATTEND

The drama began at 12:40 P.M. when Stroble, handcuffed,
was hustled up a back elevator and brought down the marble-
floored and marble-walled corridor when he arrived from
Wilshire police station. Inside the "corner pocket," the stage
had been set. Four FBI agents, who have a complaint against
Stroble for illegal flight, lurked in the background.

Stroble came through perhaps 300 spectators in the corridor. He looked on sullenly while literally scores of newspapermen's flashbulbs popped. He wore a gray suit, a dull-
green shirt, a purplish tie.

Once inside the room, Dep. Dist. Atty. Henderson began
questioning slowly but relentlessly. *Every half hour, Dist.
Atty. Simpson came out a back door to tell the progress.*
[italics added here and below]

Defendant Hesitant

At about 2:15 P.M., Simpson said, "We're getting up to the
crucial point. He's a little bit hesitant. I think he is going to
come through. I don't think there's any doubt about it."

Simpson, white-haired, was trembling.

*Television news cameras were trained on the corridor.
Radio broadcasts were made a few feet away. All telephones
in offices for 50 feet in each direction were commandeered by
newsmen.*

Death Described

Minutes ticked off. *Simpson emerged again. He told in
words of almost Biblical simplicity of Stroble's confession—
the attempted molesting, the choking, the dragging, the ice-*

pick stabbing, the ax-bludgeoning and finally the coup de
grâce, *the knifing at the back of the skull which he had learned
while watching a bullfight.*
Inside the "corner pocket" stenographers took notes in five-
minute relays and a recording machine also was used.
"I don't know how long this will continue!" Simpson said.
"We want to be sure."

Before Stroble came to trial the district attorney went to
the press again to announce that he was convinced of two
things, that Stroble was guilty, and that Stroble was sane.
And, again before the trial, District Attorney Simpson testified before a legislative committee investigating sex crimes.
He told the committee that he didn't see why sex offenders
"shouldn't be disposed of the same way" as mad dogs. At
trial, Stroble was convicted.

His attorneys appealed to the U.S. Supreme Court. Their
brief quoted the Los Angeles *Times* article and then went on
to say:

The less conservative press, like the Hearst-owned Los Angeles
Herald Express, printed the confession, and headlined the
capture of Stroble in letters two and three-eighths inches high
and three-quarters of an inch wide (Los Angeles *Herald Express,* Night Final, November 17, 1949). Nor was the coverage of the Stroble case a brief interlude lost in the mass of the
news and without mnemonic advantages of constant repetition over a period of time. The following night the *Herald
Express* announced in headlines of a size reserved by the New
York *Times* for the Second Coming, "LYNCH HIM!" HOWLS
CROWD AS STROBLE GOES TO COURT.

The same paper had dubbed the petitioner "The Werewolf" many days before his capture and many weeks before his
conviction.
Nor was the journalistic vilification of Stroble ended by his
arrest. The night edition of the *Herald Express* of November

21, 1949, carried on its front page the following account, with the subhead "Grisly Details Revealed":

The complete Answer and Question text of Werewolf-slayer Fred Stroble's confession to the fiendish murder of six-year-old Linda————. William E. Simpson today: [followed by the complete text of the confession].

The U.S. Supreme Court upheld the conviction. In its decision, the majority found that the action of the district attorney was harmless, that it did not prevent the defendant from getting a fair trial:

While we may deprecate the action of the District Attorney in releasing to the press, on the day of petitioner's arrest, certain details of the confession which petitioner made, we find that the transcript of that confession was read into the record at the preliminary hearing in the Municipal Court . . . four days later. Thus, in any event, the confession would have become available to the press at that time, for what transpires in the courtroom is "public property."

The press, of course, out of respect for justice, could have chosen not to print the confession until it became "public property."

A jury of his peers convicted Stroble. The Supreme Court affirmed the conviction. Under our law, he was proven guilty. We must assume that he was guilty, that justice was done.

Yet Justice Felix Frankfurter dissented from the Supreme Court majority. He dissented vigorously:

To have the prosecutor himself feed the press with evidence that no self-restrained press ought to publish in anticipation of a trial is to make the State itself through the prosecutor, who wields its power, a conscious participant in trial by newspaper, instead of by those methods which centuries of experience have shown to be indispensable to the fair administration of justice. Science with all its advances has not given us instruments for determining when the impact of such newspaper exploitation has spent itself or whether the powerful impressions bound to be made by such inflaming articles as here preceded the trial can be dissipated in the mind of the average juror by the tame and often pedestrian proceedings in court.

If guilt is here clear, the dignity of the law would be best enhanced by establishing that guilt wholly through the processes of law unaided by the infusion of extraneous passion. The moral health of the community is strengthened by according even the most miserable and pathetic criminal those rights which the Constitution has designed for all.

Unfortunately, even those men who have achieved the highest offices and the most honorable reputations have used the press for their own ends, when they deemed it necessary in order to win a conviction.

There is no man more respected, deservedly, than Earl Warren, Chief Justice of the United States. He enjoys an unsurpassed reputation for fairness, integrity, and regard for the rights of the individual. No one, least of all the author, would dispute that reputation.

In *Earl Warren: A Great American Story*, Irving Stone, the author of this biography written to aid Warren's 1948 campaign for the Vice-Presidency of the United States, praises Warren highly. Stone tells us that when Warren was elected district attorney of Alameda County, California, he went to the office of the public defender, Willard Shea, and said, "Willard, I know that you don't want to keep guilty men out of jail any more than I want to put innocent ones in. Therefore, I will make an agreement with you: if at any time you are convinced that we have indicted an innocent man, just come and tell me so. I will then show you my files on the case. If after looking over my material you are still convinced that the man is innocent, I will release him."

Warren kept his word and occasionally refused to prose-

cute, and released a prisoner whom Shea believed was innocent. Shea said, in 1948, "Warren never brought people into
court until he was positive they were guilty and could prove
it. He would always discuss a case with me before going into
court, rather than keeping his evidence secret so he could
spring it before a jury and thus upset or weaken my defense. I
tried a number of cases against Warren, but I never won one."

Yet Stone goes on to show that Warren, while he was district attorney, used the press to secure a conviction. He did it
purposely, openly, because he knew he could not get the conviction he wanted unless public opinion was behind him. The
following is from the same book:

A group of paving contractors in Oakland banded together
and through collusion with members of the city council obtained a monopoly on paving contracts. Not only did this
eliminate competitive bidding, but it defrauded the city out of
millions of dollars by furnishing a poor grade of paving, and
fulfilling the majority of its contracts on paper rather than on
the streets. In addition they forced all independent paving
companies out of business, and when a small home owner
wished to have a piece of sidewalk put in front of his house, it
would cost him three hundred dollars for a fifty-dollar job.
The kickbacks on the colossal graft were paid to the city
commissioner who awarded the contracts, to other city officials, and to Sheriff (Burton F.) Becker. What made the case
delicate to handle was that the contractors were now million-
aires, and represented some of the oldest and most influential
families in the community.

It was not enough for District Attorney Warren to subpoena the records and awards of the city council to the
Greater Oakland Construction Company. Neither was it adequate to subpoena the books of the paving companies and
determine how much money they had spent, and how much

work they actually had done. Nor would it be sufficient to
have the testimony only of small home owners who had been
robbed, or districts that had been forced to pay assessments
for which they had received little or no benefits. All of this
might come under the heading of bad or stupid city management. What he needed was the testimony of city officials who
had been paid off, persons who had acted as go-betweens,
men who could bring proof into court of the corruption and
conspiracy between the Oakland officials and the construction
company.

He offered immunity to the lower-paid Oakland officials
who might now be willing to make their bed on the side of the
law; the paving ring and its henchmen in government were so
powerful that no city employee dared accept. Stymied at
every turn, Warren took his records and books before the
grand jury, asking for the indictment of Commissioner of
Public Works Parker, of Sheriff Becker, of contractor Harry
Lesser. Feeling that he could not break the combine without
public support and that he had no way of getting this support
unless he could make known the grand jury testimony, *Warren released each day's proceedings to the reporters. The accused maintained that Warren acted illegally. Warren quoted
the California statute which says, " . . . members of the Grand
Jury may not disclose evidence," but does not prohibit the
district attorney from doing so.* [italics here and below added]

When the public saw the extent to which it was being victimized, and the brazenness with which it was being bilked it
turned against the elected officers and influential families and
backed the District Attorney solidly in his demand that the
grafters be brought to trial.

*"The Public never turned me down. I took my story right
to them, told them the facts bluntly, and when we got into a
pinch they stayed with us."* Now, with the pressure of public
opinion behind them, Warren was able to persuade the commissioner's office to bring him their proofs of the passage of

money from the Greater Oakland Construction Company to the public officials. Caught red-handed, Sheriff Becker resigned. But Warren promptly filed his case in the Oakland courts. . . .

Warren knew that the public grows fatigued if the big graft cases are too long and drawn out. The men under indictment knew this too and used every device, legal and otherwise, to get the cases postponed until the public would become bored with the whole affair, for then they had a good chance of beating the rap. [What difference does it make if the public becomes bored with a long and drawn out trial as long as the jury doesn't become bored?] But Warren never allowed the cases to drag or grow cold; he pushed hard, working night and day, preparing his briefs, and staying in the courts and with the judges to secure immediate trials.

The lawyers for the pavers tried delaying tactics half a dozen times, but Warren was always there in the courtroom to pose the public's legal rights against those of the ring's and the opposing attorneys never secured any of their greatly desired postponements.

Pavers and public officials alike were convicted and sent to San Quentin.

Warren's credo was always to seek justice, not convictions. If a man of his unimpeachable integrity found that he had to use the press to gain justice, what of the countless hundreds of law-enforcement officials who are more interested in convictions than in justice? To the electorate the mark of a successful district attorney is, all too frequently, the number of convictions he secures. It is the electorate that awards the district attorney with higher office if he has been a successful D. A.

The question remains: Even if a guilty verdict is deserved, is it just if it has been obtained through the pressure of public opinion inflamed by the press?

In the famed spy trial *United States v. Rosenberg,* Julius

and Ethel Rosenberg were convicted and executed for passing atomic secrets to Russia.

During the trial, attorneys for the Rosenbergs presented many witnesses in their defense. At one point *the government prosecutor was charged with deliberately making public a sealed indictment that charged one of the defense witnesses with perjury.* His intent, obviously, was to show the jury that the testimony of that witness could not be believed.

The leaked story of the perjury indictment ran in the New York *Times* on March 15, 1951, while the Rosenbergs were on trial for their lives.

The court said: "Such a statement to the press in the course of a trial is wholly reprehensible. Nevertheless we are not prepared to hold that it vitiates the jury's verdict when there is no allegation or evidence that any juror read the newspaper story."

The Rosenbergs died in the electric chair. Who is to say with certainty that no member of the jury read that story?

Leaking the story of the indictment was doubly malicious. Not only might it have influenced jurors, it might have influenced them falsely. The indictment, after all, only *accused* the witness of perjury. He might have been innocent of the accusation. At that point in the Rosenberg trial the jurors had no way of knowing. If the "reprehensible" release of that story did influence any jurors, how shall we recover our honor?

Again, the preponderant evidence indicated that the Rosenbergs were guilty. Yet if we must arrive at justice through resort to the press, the path is too crooked.

Following is another example of why no confession should be given to the press. During the week of December 17, 1962, *Newsweek* reported that Airman 1/C Gerald M. Anderson, an Air Force mechanic confessed to the April, 1962 killing of his next-door neighbor, Mrs. Nancy Johnson, and her two-year-old son, Danny. Mrs. Johnson was the pretty twenty-two-year-old wife of Anderson's Air Force buddy at Mountain Home Air Force Base in North Dakota.

Nine months later, Theodore Thomas Dickie, twenty-one, also confessed to the same crime. But he did so in such detail that he left no doubt that he was the actual murderer. At the time of his confession, Dickie was in a North Dakota penitentiary on charges of raping and killing a ten-year-old girl.

Authorities asked Anderson why he had confessed. The veteran of service in Saudi Arabia and Okinawa, who had been awarded the Good Conduct ribbon, told a story that should make anyone doubt the validity of a confession that has not been tested at a trial. Anderson explained that he simply broke down after repeated questioning. He had been interrogated for over 40 hours over a period of eight days. "Every time I said I didn't do it," Anderson recalled, "one of the investigators would say, 'I don't want to hear that. We've already crossed that bridge.'" Anderson finally confessed to a crime he didn't commit because, he explained, "I was so tired and confused from the continued prolonged questioning and badgering that I felt that anything was better than the continued questioning and harassment I had gone through."

In the light of possibilities like this, it is difficult to accept any confession at face value. Certainly it is difficult to believe that a confession establishes guilt "beyond reasonable doubt."

Why, then, do public officials persist in leaking them to the press? And why does the press persist in publishing them?

On November 16, 1964, the Supreme Court of the state of New Jersey took a revolutionary step forward. It ordered a ban on potentially prejudicial statements by prosecutors, policemen, and defense lawyers to news media before and during trials.

The court singled out as prejudicial any prosecution or police statements about "alleged confessions or inculpatory admissions" by an accused person, any statement that a case was "open and shut," and references to a defendant's prior police record.

The court said that this ban could be enforced against prosecutors and defense attorneys through the court's power of discipline under the canons of professional ethics. It further said that improper statements by a policeman should be dealt with by superior officers as conduct unbecoming a policeman. This is a fatal weakness. Police tend to protect each other just as do physicians, lawyers, and other members of specific groups.

This decision, important as it is, does not provide for action against the news media for making public information that the court might consider prejudicial. The way is left open for continued leaks, for stories ascribed to "informed sources," since there is no way for the court to learn who released the information to the press if it is released *sub rosa*. In New Jersey and in many other states reporters are not required to reveal the sources of their information.

The case that prompted this decision involved the murder of his wife by one Louis Van Duyne, in Passaic County, N.J. Van Duyne's attorney showed the Supreme Court of New Jersey that copies of the October 7, 1963, Paterson *Evening News* had been found in the jurors' assembly room, and that that newspaper, in describing Van Duyne's capture, said, "Police quoted him as saying, 'You've got me for murder. I don't desire to tell you anything.'"

(Although the New Jersey court found Van Duyne's case

so upsetting that it enunciated its new rule, it did not order a new trial for Van Duyne. He will be electrocuted unless the U.S. Supreme Court reverses the decision.

(It is ironic that Van Duyne's memorial will be a case that bears his name and enunciates a doctrine that will prevent prejudicial publicity from harming others, but which helped him not at all.)

In its directive the court also said: "Unfair and prejudicial newspaper stories and comment both before and during trial of criminal cases are becoming more and more prevalent throughout the country."

The court quoted a decision by Justice Felix Frankfurter, in a U.S. Supreme Court case, in which Justice Frankfurter suggested that "inflammatory" pre-trial newspaper stories are published "too often . . . with the prosecutor's collaboration."

The decision said, too:

An answer to problems such as are presented here must be achieved. Fair criminal prosecution and exercise of the guarantee of a free press are not incompatible with the constitutional right of a defendant to a fair trial by an impartial jury. Only the will to recognize and subscribe responsibly to that fact has been lacking.

This is a landmark decision, productive of great hope that accused persons will receive fairer treatment in the future. Yet the decision is tempered by the divisions in our land. Each state sets its own rules in matters of this sort. New Jersey is only one of fifty states. What happens to the defendant in those states where the courts have not yet been willing to accord him this protection?

The time for counting the problem solved is far off. Newspapers continue to compete in the area of reporting crime news. The day after the New Jersey Supreme Court delivered its opinion, the New York *Times* editorialized:

The New Jersey ruling seems to us to place the main bur-
den of responsibility where it belongs—on the officials and
members of the bar who disclose pre-trial information. This is
a much more promising approach than exhortations to television and to the press to exercise voluntary self-restraint. Such
appeals are usually ignored in the harsh competition to get the
news.

It will be recalled that District Attorney Hogan issued a
similar edict, that the New York *Times* published a similar
editorial, and that the problem continued unabated.

To protect the honorable members of the press from the
unfair competition of its not-so-honorable members, perhaps
all the press must be enjoined legally, with stiff penalties for
violations, from publishing leaked or openly given information until a trial is ended.

FOUR

The ABC's of Circulation

WHEN news was light I can recall the city desk rounding up every one of the night's purse-snatchings, two-bit break ins, trivial cutting scrapes and vagrancy arrests and emerging on the street with a flaming banner-line reading: CRIME WAVE SWEEPS CITY. And if at eleven o'clock in the morning we got a decent news story the crime wave fell out of the paper and nobody ever referred to it again.

So wrote Norman E. Isaacs, managing editor of the Louisville *Times*, of the days when he was a beginning reporter.

The University of Pennsylvania *Law Review* wrote:

Without it [juvenile delinquency] many American newspapers might have gone into receivership. It has even been reported that newspapers were instrumental in pressing for the repeal of the New York Youth Court Act: "Newspaper publishers were against the bill because it would have thrown a veil of secrecy around the criminal acts of youth."

Additional corroboration of some publishers' less than idealistic interest in crime comes from Albert Colegrove, western correspondent for the Scripps-Howard newspapers. In his article "Attitudes Toward Crime News—A Newspaperman's Viewpoint," he points out that on the day in 1957 that

[98]

a man named Burton Abbott was executed for the murder of a young girl—Stephanie Bryan—the circulation of the San Francisco *News* went up 20,000 copies. The circulation fell off again the next day.

Also in 1957, according to Colegrove, a young terrorist, wielding a knife, attacked a couple in a car in Golden Gate Park. He tied up the man, manacled the girl, then assaulted, tortured, and beat her, and finally shaved her head.

The police quickly arrested a suspect. Newspaper stories during the next three weeks indicated that he was the rapist. Then the police caught another suspect, who, it turned out, was the real rapist.

During the three weeks that this story was front-page news, the circulation of the San Francisco newspapers rose 15,000 daily.

In 1954, *Time* published a story on the relationship between the sensationalism in the reporting of the Dr. Sam Sheppard trial and newspaper circulation. The story quoted managing editor Herbert Krauch, of the Los Angeles *Herald and Express:* "It's been a long time since there's been a murder trial this good."

In connection with the same case *Time* also reported an extreme example of the mercenary use of crime news to boost circulation:

Even before the trial got under way, some editors decided it was going to be the biggest crime story in years. Publisher William R. Hearst, Jr., who has been trying to jack up his ailing chain, saw the trial as a rare opportunity. He ordered a task force dispatched to Cleveland led by Sob Sister Dorothy Kilgallen, Handyman Bob Considine, and Cartoonist Burris Jenkins, Jr. Scripps-Howard followed suit with its own crew. . . .

People go into business to make a profit, newspaper owners included. The press, no less than General Motors or the local supermarket, hates to show an unfavorable balance sheet. John Hay Whitney is not pumping millions into the New York *Herald Tribune* only because he wants to preserve a tradition. If that were his reason the *Trib* might still be stodgy. It is significant that the *Tribune's* new slogan, after Whitney took over, became: "Who says a good newspaper has to be dull?" Front-page crime stories are part of the *Tribune's* formula to conquer dullness.

Newspapers have tested their markets thoroughly. They've had centuries to find out what the public wants to read. They found out that the public responds to sex and crime stories, and that is what it gets. (It is always mystifying to hear a newspaper accuse television of pandering to public taste.)

Why, then, are newspapers closing down? Why are there more one-paper cities than ever before, if the press is so efficient at determining and providing what the public wants? Simply put, a crime is a crime. There is no need to read about it in four different newspapers; one will do. An excellent example of this is the demise of Hearst's New York *Mirror* in 1964. The *Mirror* and the New York *Daily News* were the city's most racy papers. No crime was too small, if bloody enough, for their splashy coverage. But both papers covered the same crimes, the same adulteries, the same rumbles. The public chose the *News*.

The first law of the circulation manager, then, is: crime makes news and crime news makes readers. This wouldn't necessarily be bad if one could write about crime without writing about the people who commit—or allegedly commit—the crimes. It is in the cause of these people that press privilege must be re-examined.

The press on its own very rarely makes any accusations, or exposes any of the chicanery going on in Washington. Yet in off-the-record conversations with the most knowledgeable reporters and columnists in that city, one hears documented stories of governmental corruption that defy belief. Why, if the press is so interested in the preservation of democracy, does it attack the accused criminal whose only defense is the Constitution? Why does it not attack and expose lawmakers who use their offices, sometimes even flaunting their use of these offices, illegally and for personal gain?

A pertinent example of just this is the Bobby Baker story. Baker had been a poor boy from Pickens, South Carolina, before he came to Washington. Only a few years later he had risen to become secretary to the Senate majority. On the way he managed to acquire part ownership of a luxurious motel near Washington. He became, too, a major stockholder in corporations doing business with big defense contractors, and he owned a very expensive home in a very expensive suburb. Senator Williams of Delaware accused him of influence peddling and conflict of interest.

During the weeks when the Senate committee was investigating the charges against Bobby Baker, the National Educational Television network was filming a documentary on *Justice and the Press*. A camera crew was sent out to interview people in two sections of New York City, to find out what effect press treatment of Bobby Baker had on the reading public.

Foley Square, legal center of New York City, was the first stop. Thirty people, all of whom had some professional connection with the legal profession, were asked, "Have you followed the newspaper and television accounts of the Bobby Baker investigation?" All thirty had. When they were asked if they thought Bobby Baker was guilty of something, twelve of the thirty immediately said, "Yes." Two of the twelve were lawyers, four were court clerks, and the others were secretaries and messengers. Despite their relationship to the law, despite their daily contact with the "innocent till proven guilty" basis of criminal law, twelve people said Bobby Baker was guilty. Even worse, they couldn't define the crime of which he was guilty. They only knew he was guilty of something.

None of them had been to Washington to attend the hearings. None of them knew any of the principals involved in the investigation. No law-enforcement agency of any kind had made any official charges against Bobby Baker. The only information that any of these people had was what was available to all of us—the information that came from the press. On that basis, twelve out of thirty people were prepared to convict Bobby Baker of criminal activity.

All thirty, however, had worked in and around the legal profession. As a control, to ascertain whether or not these legal connections in any way acted as a restraint, as a guide line for responsibility, the camera crew went to Washington Square, in New York City.

Washington Square is the heart of Greenwich Village. In it, at any time of day, one finds New York University students, retired professional people, young and middle-aged housewives, and the large number of beatniks who are an expected part of the Greenwich Village scene.

Again, thirty people were interviewed. This time anyone who had any connection with the law was weeded out. This eliminated one retired lawyer, two wives of lawyers, a law student, the wife of a policeman, and a process server. Of the thirty interviewed, seven were university students, six were housewives, two were faculty members at New York University, one was a taxi driver, three were out-of-work advertising men, four were writers, two were baby nurses, three were park maintenance men, and two were physicians.

All thirty, every one of them, thought Bobby Baker was guilty. Two thought he was guilty of bribery, but they had no idea who bribed whom. Seven or eight thought he was guilty of influence peddling. The rest just thought he was guilty. Not one of the thirty would have been an impartial juror. Every one of the thirty had formed his opinions from stories in the press, and "the way he [Bobby Baker] looked on television." Nine months later, as this is written, Bobby Baker has still not been officially accused of any crime.

In August, 1962, New Yorkers were horrified when two young career girls were attacked and stabbed to death early one morning in their own luxury apartment on the fashionable East Side of the city. The crime was bloody and vicious enough to attract headlines of the size usually reserved for declarations of war. Multiple stabbings, nude corpses, head wounds caused by a blunt instrument, two attractive girls— all the ingredients needed for a sensational story were there. In addition, one of the girls, Janice Wylie, was the actress daughter of a well-known writer-ad man (Max Wylie), the niece of an even more famous novelist (Philip Wylie). Her roommate, Emily Hoffert, the other murdered girl, had come to New York seeking a career, leaving a small town in Wisconsin for the sophistication of the big city. This had all the makings of a big story, and a big story it became.

The story of the Wylie-Hoffert murders screamed for readers, and got them. All the gory details were described— the condition of the girls, the overturned, ransacked apartment, the speculation about the murder weapon. Nothing was left unsaid, even less was left to the imagination.

The story ran in all the New York papers, and in many other papers, for several days. Every day there were new details, new quotes from the police, sorrowful statements from the parents of the girls.

New Yorkers living in the area of the killings hired extra guards. Police assigned additional patrolmen to the area. Apartment buildings strengthened their security precautions. Closed-circuit-television cameras were installed in self-service elevators in many apartment buildings. This was all reported by the newspapers.

The city was ready for vengeance. Even if the murderer were not to be caught for months, the city would not that soon forget the horror of the double murders, and its fear of the one who committed them.

There was no dearth of news in August, 1962, when the two girls were murdered. There might have been a shortage of circulation-building news, but there was no shortage of legitimate material for the papers to print. Instead, the press roused the city into fury against an unknown killer.

My quarrel is not that the press carried the story. It had a legitimate right and an obligation to warn the public. But the lurid writing, the scare technique had nothing to do with warning the public. It was classic circulation building through a classic murder case. New York City has several bloody murders every day. Yet almost all of these go unreported. Obviously, if the prime purpose of stories like those on the Wylie-Hoffert murders is to warn the public, all the murders would be handled in the same sensational fashion. Certainly, one murderer is as dangerous as another.

In April, 1962, eight months after the murders, the New York police captured George Whitmore, Jr., nineteen, on suspicion of an attempted rape in Brooklyn. They took him to headquarters for questioning. The victim of the attempted rape identified him. Then, according to newspaper stories, the questioning shifted "routinely" to other crimes. During this "routine" questioning, police said, he admitted slaying a Mrs. Minnie Edmonds. Then, again according to the police—who told newspaper reporters—he confessed that he killed Janice Wylie and Emily Hoffert.

It became the number-one story on newscasts, the banner story for newspapers.

(As the press well knew, Whitmore was captured by the police, identified by his supposed victim, and made his three confessions *before* he saw a lawyer.)

The mildest story appeared in the New York *Times.* Its headline said: YOUTH IS ACCUSED IN WYLIE SLAYING. THEFT SUSPECT CHARGED WITH KILLING 2 CAREER GIRLS IN EAST SIDE APARTMENT.

The article ran:

A slender, near-sighted 19-year-old drifter in the Brownsville section of Brooklyn was charged yesterday with stabbing Janice Wylie and Emily Hoffert to death in their East Side apartment last August.

The police said [italics added here and throughout article] the suspect, George Whitmore, had admitted killing the two career girls. *They said* he also had confessed to the slaying of a Brooklyn woman on April 14.

The chain of events, *as outlined by Chief of Detectives Lawrence J. McKearney,* began on Thursday, when a young women was attacked on a Brooklyn street.

The next morning, cruising the area looking for a suspect, three policemen saw Whitmore standing on a corner. They picked him up and took him to a station for questioning. That's where the *victim identified Whitmore* as her attacker, and that's where the questioning shifted "routinely" to other crimes.

Whitmore was asked about the murder of Mrs. Minnie

Edmonds. Her deeply slashed body had been found in a back-yard at 444 Blake Avenue in Brownsville on April 14.

He reportedly confessed readily. No motive was disclosed. Late Friday night Whitmore was taken in handcuffs to the East New York station. The questioning continued there.

The youth, a Negro, carried snapshots of two unidentified young women, both white. According to detectives, Whitmore had told acquaintances that the two were "girl friends."

Detective Edward Bolger of the Brooklyn North homicide squad was present at the questioning. He had been assigned to the Wylie case until the end of December.

Because of the two photographs—and the similarity of the crimes—Mr. Bolger then asked Whitmore if he knew anything about the death of the two young women on the East Side.

Still impassive, *according to Chief McKearney,* and speaking in a soft, halting voice, he admitted the crime.

His confession, given to Peter Koste, a New York County assistant district attorney, was said to have included *details that have not been made public.* These details were not **disclosed.**

At this point the *Times* story, still attributing its information to Chief McKearney, traced Whitmore's path on August 28 from a subway station in Times Square to the girls' apartment. The story says he entered the building only by chance, intending to go up to the roof to have a look around. Again by chance, according to the chief of detectives, he stopped at the third floor, tried several apartment doors before finding that the door to 3-C was unlocked.

Intent on robbery, detectives believe, he entered.

The suspect's statement to the police said that he was rummaging around in the kitchen of the apartment at about 10 A.M. when Miss Wylie, wearing only a towel, walked out of the bathroom. She was the only one of the three [roommates] at home, and was due to report to the magazine office at 11.

The young woman saw Whitmore and screamed, *according to the police.* He told the police he picked up a soft-drink bottle from the floor of the kitchen and struck her with it, knocking her unconscious. He then tied her hands and feet and dragged her to the bedroom, he stated.

It was the room that Miss Hoffert occupied alone. A clock radio was stopped at 10:35 and police believe that that was the hour at which Whitmore stabbed Miss Wylie repeatedly with one of three knives taken from the kitchen.

Miss Hoffert had left the apartment at about 9:30 A.M. to return a car she had borrowed a few days earlier to Riverdale, the Bronx. . . .

She left Riverdale at about 11 A.M. *detectives said,* and was believed to have reached her apartment about thirty minutes later. Whitmore reportedly told his questioners that when Miss Hoffert returned he knocked her out with a soft-drink bottle, tied her, and continued to ransack the apartment.

"Another girl came into the apartment and saw me," *Chief McKearney quoted the suspect as saying.* [This quote referred to Miss Hoffert.]

But Miss Hoffert regained consciousness and began to cry for help, according to the police. The *police said Whitmore* then apparently dragged her to the bedroom and slashed her repeatedly in the head and throat.

The force of the attack broke the blades of two of the three knives.

"Then," *Chief McKearney said,* "he calmly washed his hands and left as he had entered."

There was a strong undercurrent of elation when *Deputy Police Commissioner Walter Arm* [in charge of public relations] *announced Whitmore's confession at 3:30 A.M. yesterday, and as Chief McKearney gave the details of the suspect's statements.*

Whitmore, who is 5-feet-5 and weighs about 140 pounds, wore a striped blue, black, and white sweater, slacks and sports shirt as he stood before Judge James J. Comerford, surrounded by detectives and reporters in the old Criminal Courts Building at 120 Schermerhorn Street, Brooklyn.

The judge, who speaks with a marked and musical brogue, asked the suspect if he had a lawyer. "No," he replied. Judge Comerford then appointed Mr. Leftow to represent him.

They conferred privately and when they returned Mr. Leftow said, "My client has made certain statements to the police. These statements and confessions were made under duress and stress and he now recants all the confessions he made."

Thus did the New York *Times*, most responsible of all the nation's newspapers, give a play-by-play account of the police-department version of a brutal murder. The suspect had not yet faced a grand jury. He was grilled by the police before he saw a lawyer, and his statements were flashed to the reading public by an eager press. The story was filled with, indeed it was based on, quotations and statements from the police—statements that probably would be used as evidence in court. It was used as evidence for the public first. There's not much justice, but lots of circulation in stories like that.

The press, of course, was careful to preface most allusions to the suspect with the words "alleged slayer" or some such libel-evading phrase. The press is as careful to avoid a libel suit as it is careless about the rights of a possibly innocent man. That was the sole extent of the press protection of the rights of George Whitmore to a fair trial—the use of the word "alleged."

An easy defense for the press to use is to point out that it printed, too, the boy's recantation of his confession. How many people, though, reading the details in the story above, would choose to believe the recantation?

The next day, the New York *World-Telegram & Sun* ran

this headline: WYLIE SUSPECT FACES QUIZ IN N.J. KILLING. The
story ran on:

George Whitmore, Jr., 19, charged with the knife murders
of two Manhattan career girls and a Brooklyn woman, was to
be questioned today about a similar slaying in New Jersey.
Newark detectives were to ask him about the kidnap murder of Mrs. Eleanor Lynch, 27, of Iselin. Kidnaped at knife-
point from a Woodbridge motel where she was night clerk,
Mrs. Lynch was driven to Newark last January 3, and murdered in the basement of an apartment building in the fashionable Forest Hills section.
Her body, nude except for a bra, was found tied by her
hands to a water pipe. She had been raped, strangled, and
stabbed 62 times.
*The Woodbridge motel is on a main road that young
Whitmore often traveled between New York and his parents'
home in Wildwood, N.J.* [italics added]

Further in the story, referring to Whitmore's recantation of
his confession of the Wylie-Hoffert murders, we read:

But a police-department spokesman said: "This man came
up with details that could have been known by no one but the
police and the killer. He had information that had never been
revealed publicly!"

And what of the other obvious parallel the *World-Telegram* planted in its story—the fact that the New Jersey murder and the Wylie-Hoffert murders were both effected by
seemingly insane stabbings?

Evidently newspapers don't consult the rules of morality
when they're going after another thousand readers.

The New York *Journal-American*, also on Monday, April
27, quoted the police as citing a dozen points in Whitmore's
statement, several unpublished by any other newspaper, that
convinced them he had committed the Wylie-Hoffert killings.

The points included locating a razor blade on a bedroom floor and the blade's wrapper on a bathroom sink (the razor was allegedly used to cut a bedspread to gag the girls); describing the lid of a jar of Noxema cream left on the bed, with the open jar on the floor; reporting some bloodstains on a bedroom shade; placing two handles of broken knives on a radiator cover; describing a bedsheet under the bodies as blue.

Asked about the *Journal-American* article, Deputy Police Commissioner Walter Arm said, "It is not an official statement. It was not issued by this department. I have no comment beyond statements made the first day."

The New York *Times*, on Tuesday, April 28, pointed out that Whitmore was accused of a murder in Manhattan and a murder in Brooklyn, and that, consequently, he came under the jurisdiction of two different district attorneys. Brooklyn's District Attorney Edward Silver said he expected that both his office and Mr. Hogan's would seek indictments in the murders, and thereafter would "determine where the case is tried first, solely on the basis of what is best for the people."

Mr. Whitmore is one of the people. Why didn't Mr. Silver consider that before he allowed the press to run statements about his prisoner? Yet an even more valid question is, why didn't the press consider that Mr. Whitmore was one of the people?

The New York *Daily News* gave its readers their sevencents' worth by including a direct quote from Chief McKearney: "He finally broke down and made a full confession."

The *News* went on to say:

However, court-appointed defense attorney Jerome Leftow of Brooklyn promptly announced that the prisoner was repudiating all his admissions to the cops.

Police insisted, however, that Whitmore . . . knew intimate details of the Wylie-Hoffert murders *and perversions that preceded them* [italics added] that would have been known only to the slayer and investigators.

The reason for the venom struck at the press in this chapter becomes all too apparent in what follows.

The New York *Daily News*, Monday, November 2, 1964:

D.A. Confirms New Angle on Girls' Murder: The Manhattan District Attorney's office yesterday confirmed an exclusive story in the *Sunday News* that a possible new suspect has been turned up in the double murder of Janice Wylie and Emily Hoffert. A 19-year-old drifter, George Whitmore, Jr., is now under indictment in the killings.

The New York *Post*, Monday, November 2, 1964:

Cops Waiting 2nd Man's Story in Wylie Case: Police today waited outside a metropolitan hospital room to question an ex-convict named as the killer of career girls Janice Wylie and Emily Hoffert.
The 21-year-old suspect is suffering from an apparent overdose of narcotics. He was brought to the hospital three weeks ago, and is in critical condition.

Also according to the *Post*, the new suspect went to the apartment of a friend the day of the Wylie-Hoffert murders, covered with blood. He told his friend he had killed the two girls, and gave details of the twin murders.

The *Post* helps Whitmore, but doesn't do the new suspect any good. Why not, after all, make the same mistake twice?

As the weeks passed, other evidence that the police had claimed (and the newspapers had printed) proving Whitmore's guilt fell apart.

When the police arrested Whitmore, they said he was carrying a photograph of the two murdered girls. Soon it became a photograph of just one girl. And then, in January, 1965—nine months after Whitmore's arrest and all the publicity—it developed that the photograph was of neither murdered girl, but of a girl from his home town, 120 miles from New York. Yet every New York City newspaper had reported the police story that Whitmore had been found carrying photographs of the two murdered girls.

Despite the unanswered questions that kept popping up, the Brooklyn district attorney, in the fall of 1964, decided to bring Whitmore to trial on the attempted-rape charge. Much of the prosecution's case was based on a button torn by the victim from the attacker's coat. It was identified as matching buttons on a coat owned by Whitmore. The newspapers printed that information, too.

In November, 1964, Whitmore was convicted. In January, 1965, the FBI conducted laboratory tests to determine whether or not the button used in evidence came from George Whitmore's coat. The FBI reported that its tests *failed* to show that the button definitely came from Whitmore's coat.

One must wonder whether Whitmore was convicted on the basis of such lackluster evidence—or on the basis of the stories that appeared in the press.

In arguing for a new trial, Whitmore's lawyers introduced an affidavit from one of the jurors in the trial stating that "racial and other prejudicial statements were made by other jurors during the trial." *His lawyers also charged that jurors had discussed Whitmore's alleged confession and indictment in the murder of career girls Janice Wylie and Emily Hoffert.* These jurors could not have discussed the alleged confession if news of it, released by the police, had not appeared in the newspapers.

Whitmore's lawyers, with ample precedent, claim too, that

it is extremely rare for a person accused of two separate crimes, one more serious than the other, to be tried first for the less serious crime. They point out that it is almost always the more serious crime that comes to trial first.

These lawyers maintain that the murder case against Whitmore was very weak, and that consequently the authorities decided to get a conviction on the attempted-rape charge before the murder case came to court. This would then have enabled the prosecution in the murder case to point to Whitmore as a convicted attempted rapist—a fact bound to sway any jury. (This would have been admissible because Whitmore would, inevitably, have taken the witness stand in his own defense. Once a defendant does this, any prior criminal record becomes admissible.)

As events turned out, Whitmore may have been very lucky indeed that he was accused of the attempted rape. If he had not been, he might have been tried immediately on the murder charge. At that time the evidence against him had not been broken down, and New Yorkers were still very much under the influence of all the newspaper stories which had printed the original police and district attorney statements.

The Whitmore case was to take on yet additional overtones, frightening because of new press involvement, and encouraging because of a legal decision. In early February, 1965, all the communications media of New York City reported a new arrest for the murders of Janice Wylie and Emily Hoffert.

WNBC-TV announced that Richard Robles, *a narcotics addict with a long record of burglary arrests,* had been charged with the murders.

The headline in the New York *Times* read:

PAROLEE BOOKED
IN WYLIE SLAYING
ADDICT HELD IN DOUBLE KILLING
—PROSECUTOR IS SILENT ON
WHITMORE INDICTMENT

The New York *Herald Tribune* headline read:

SECOND SUSPECT BOOKED
IN WYLIE CASE MURDERS

Both newspapers, as did all radio and television stations in New York, emphasized that Robles was a narcotics addict and ex-convict.

The *Herald Tribune* also quoted Robles as telling a friend, after the murders, "I iced those two dames."

When the press asked District Attorney Hogan for comment, he replied, "I refuse to comment, and if anybody in my shop comments, he'll be discharged."

Where, then, did the *Herald Tribune* get the quote it attributed to Robles?

When the press tried to ask Chief of Detectives McKearney for a comment, he couldn't be found. McKearney was the man who told the press, when Whitmore was arrested, "He's the man all right—we wouldn't have booked him unless we were sure."

The New York *Times* said Robles spends "about $15 a day" for heroin. The *Herald Tribune* said Robles spends "$30 to $50 a day" for heroin. Which newspaper does a prospective juror believe?

History was repeating itself. The press treated Robles just as it had treated Whitmore. Finally, in March of 1965, New York Supreme Court Justice David L. Malbin threw out Whitmore's conviction on the attempted-rape charge.

In his decision, Justice Malbin said:

The widespread publicity reported by the press, television coverage and radio contributed in no slight degree to the atmosphere of hostility that surrounded Whitmore's trial.

Whitmore was the victim of injustice. Prejudice and racial bias invaded the jury room. Bigotry cannot be permitted to gain a foothold in our democratic institutions. . . .

Much controversy exists among the judiciary, bar associations and representatives of the press concerning the problem of fair dissemination of news, relating to the arrest and trial of those accused of crime.

It is inescapable that they must bear some blame for the unfavorable widespread publicity concerning this defendant which made it extremely difficult, if not impossible, that the verdict was uninfluenced by the incessant, inflammatory reports that branded the defendant as the confessor of three unrelated homicides.

The press will never respect the rights of an individual until it is forced to—by law.

FIVE

The Reporter's Diligence,
the Defendant's Sentence

IN NOVEMBER, 1964, Federal Judge Jacob Mishler was presiding over a trial, in Brooklyn, New York, of seven men accused of conspiracy to loot several U.S. Post Offices.

The prosecution had introduced a witness to testify against the defendants. The defense attorney, recognizing in advance that the testimony might be prejudicial and thus inadmissible, asked the judge to excuse the jury while the prosecution offered proof as to what the forthcoming testimony would be. He knew that, once it was given in front of the jury, even if afterward ruled inadmissible, the testimony would have left an indelible impression on the jury.

Judge Mishler excused the jury, and the prosecutor outlined the nature of the testimony. Immediately, the defense attorney stated that, in his opinion, it *would* be inflammatory and prejudicial. Not yet certain how he would rule on its admissibility, Judge Mishler decided to delay the testimony of the witness until a later date.

Aware that jurors, despite instructions not to read newspapers, often read them anyway, the judge asked the only reporter present, a representative from the New York *Times*, whether he intended to use the defense attorney's statement that the testimony was prejudicial, saying, "I certainly don't want it to appear in print."

Despite the request of the court not to print the verbatim statement, the reporter paraphrased the statement and ran the story. To add insult to injury, the reporter characterized the judge as a man of "high reputation in the Eastern District as a careful, thorough legal expert, who 'bends over backwards' to protect a defendant's interests."

One week later in the same trial, Judge Mishler again excused the jurors to avoid their hearing potentially prejudical testimony. The reporter, nevertheless, quoted that testimony in his story the next day:

It was also said, in the absence of the jury, that Guzzo had a grenade concealed in his home. This explosive, carefully placed in a small drawer as a booby trap, could have killed a United States marshal or postal officer inspecting the house.

In his eagerness to use his big story, the reporter was evidently able to convince himself, however naïvely, that all jurors follow their instructions not to read newspaper accounts of trial proceedings.

Any juror who read either of these New York *Times* stories would, inevitably, have been influenced by them to the detriment of the defendant. Of whatever importance or interest it was to the public to read the stories, it would have been just as interesting, and less hazardous to the defendant, to read them *after* the trial.

If proof is needed that jurors do read newspaper stories relating to the trial they sit in judgment in, it is provided by *People v. Lyng*, in Minneapolis, Minnesota.

Donald Lyng was charged with swindling. While his trial was in progress, the following story appeared in a local newspaper:

'I'M BORROWER, NOT SWINDLER,' "ROMEO" SAYS

A 31-year-old man, charged with swindling a Minneapolis mother of five out of $1,335, denied in Hennepin County District Court Monday that he is a swindler.

Donald M. Lyng . . . said he only borrowed the money from Mrs. Gertrude Crimmins, 312 South Eighth Street, a former pianist at a loop bar.

Police previously said some 15 women claimed Lyng loved them, but left with their money—a total of close to $25,000. He is being tried on one charge. . . .

A 27-year-old Bloomington woman told the court how Lyng had sold her car and used the money to take her on a jaunt to California and Florida. . . .

Lyng was arrested on an illegitimacy charge by a third woman after returning to Minneapolis in October."

The defense, learning that at least one juror had read the story, moved for a mistrial. It was granted.

No one will argue that the possibility of a juror reading a newspaper account of a trial was limited to one case in Hennepin County, Minnesota.

In *People v. Nicholas P. Brooks,* a murder trial in Rochester, New York, the defense asked that the trial be moved to another area, arguing that great amounts of prejudicial opinion had appeared in the local newspapers. Mr. Brooks was accused of killing his wife by drowning her in Lake Ontario.

Denying the request, the judge wrote in his opinion:

The facts of the case were such as to afford plenty of material for sensational "write-ups" by the press, and interesting speculation by the public as to the guilt or innocence of the defendant. It is a matter of common knowledge that newspapers and certain other types of publications are prone to present every possible detail of a case involving murder. . . . In the instant case there undoubtedly was much talk and speculation by the public as the day to day accounts appeared concerning the murder, the search for the alleged killer, his capture, etc. . . .

Defendant's counsel particularly stresses the fact that a reporter, who wrote a number of the newspaper articles and is employed by the owners of Rochester's two and only daily newspapers, flew in a plane owned by his employers to Fort Wayne, Indiana, in company with an officer of the Rochester Police Department, and the chief photographer for said newspaper owners, where they picked up the defendant and a man with him, and flew them back to Rochester. While the acceptance of the police of assistance of this character from the newspaper publishers of Rochester seems quite unusual, this Court is unable to find how the factual reporting of such action could or did incite hatred and prejudice against the defendant. . . .

However subjective the opinion, the defense had to abide by it. Other judges in other areas have granted motions for changes of venue in similar circumstances. It was impossible, actually, for that judge—or any judge—to know how such stories affect the minds of potential jurors. If the reporter had been under legal restraint with respect to the information he could print, the problem would not have existed. There should be no reason for any reporter, anywhere, to place a judge in a situation requiring a subjective and therefore possibly unjust decision.

One judge who, in an even less sensational case in a much bigger city, did grant a motion for a change of locale was Judge Irving R. Kaufman. Because the case was less sensational and the city—New York—about forty times larger than Rochester, another judge might have argued that the press had much less effect. The decision is always up to one fallible, human judge. In his opinion granting the motion, Judge Kaufman wrote:

I emphasize that this case was to proceed to trial and the selection of a jury on the morning of December 16. On that very morning, in connection with the preliminary motion for change of venue, there was placed in evidence an article appearing in the New York *World-Telegram* dated September 15 and articles appearing in the New York *Daily News,* New York *Mirror,* New York *Times* and New York *Herald Tribune* dated December 16. Some of these stories described the defendant as a "mobster" and leader of a notorious organization known as the "Ed Florio gang." Frequent mention was made of the fact that defendant was an ex-convict and repeated reference was made to events and accusations which associated the defendant with crimes bearing no relation to the present indictment. Of particular importance was the fact that this avalanche of publicity, with bold headlines concerning "dock racketeering" and Florio himself, reached the public on the very morning when the jury was to be impaneled. . . . The court cannot ignore the constitutional safeguards placed around a defendant. . . .

Judge Kaufman was concerned that the efforts of reporters had negated constitutional safeguards. But how effective are those safeguards if a judge in Rochester differs from a judge in New York on the effects of pre-trial publicity? Possibly one judge was right, and the other wrong. Yet neither would have had to make such a decision if the reporters involved had not written the stories *when* they did.

Who had the fairer trial, Mr. Brooks, who was tried in Rochester, or Mr. Florio, who was tried in Washington, D.C. —almost 300 miles from New York, the city where he received so much publicity?

In September, 1964, in New York City, Mr. I. A. Silva was in jail awaiting trial for murder. By a strange quirk a completely different case, a $100,000 injury suit brought by the same Mr. Silva, for injuries sustained in an automobile accident, came to court while Silva was waiting for his murder trial to begin.

The automobile-injury suit required Silva to testify in court, before a jury. The presiding justice in that case, Charles Marks, did not want the jurors to know that Silva was a defendant in a murder case. Yet Silva could not be allowed to go to court "unescorted." He might have tried to escape.

Accordingly, before the jurors were brought in, Silva was taken to court handcuffed and accompanied by two guards wearing pistols. The guards were not wearing jackets; thus their pistols, in shoulder holsters, would have been easily visible to the jurors. Taking precautions so that the jurors would not be prejudiced by seeing Mr. Silva handcuffed and surrounded by armed guards, Justice Marks ordered the handcuffs removed, and substituted two other guards, wearing jackets.

At the close of that day's court session, Justice Marks *admonished all the jurors not to read any newspaper accounts of the case* and told them that they would have to return to court the next day—September 24.

On the evening of September 23, and the morning of September 24, many hours before court reopened, reporter Jack Roth reported the full story in the New York *Times.*

If even one juror had disobeyed the court's instructions, Justice Marks's efforts would have been wasted—and all because a reporter decided that his interests, and those of his newspaper, were more important than the intent of a court of justice.

En route to the top, beginning reporters are frequently assigned to cover police stations. It is from the cell block that they graduate, hopefully, to the press rooms of the State Department, Congress, and the White House. It is while looking over the shoulder of the booking sergeant that they must become potential Pulitzer Prize winners. This is where they break into print, where cubs become bears, where the world of journalism will catch its first sight of a new star in the newspaper heaven.

Consider the attitude of the police themselves—police who have been on the force for years, exposed to all kinds of crime so often that the only difference between a murderer and a pickpocket is the spelling. Most police think "guilty."

These police and these reporters spend their working days together. The combination does not foster objectivity.

Then there is the prisoner. When he is brought in for booking, there is no mistaking him for Little Lord Fauntleroy. He looks atrocious. The circumstance of being in custody, rightly or wrongly, hardly contributes to the guiltless look. He is dressed for a "come as you are" party, with perhaps a bit more disarray arranged by his captors. He is sullen, angry, fearful, and surrounded by men in blue. Very likely he has also been handcuffed. Above all is the knowledge, in the minds of all those watching, that he was picked up and brought in for *something*.

The scenery hurts, too. Most police stations have never known the touch of a decorator. Overhead are old-fashioned, dim lights; on the walls the paint is so old it needs medicare; scarred, burned, chipped furniture, bars on the windows, and unpainted, bare, wooden floors complete the scene. Everything about the scene says, "Guilty." All this is before a word has been said about the crime the prisoner is supposed to have committed.

In the middle, handcuffed, alone, uncertain, fenced in by men with clubs and guns, facing a desk officer who asks, "Ya ever been arrested before?" stands the prisoner. *Accused* of a crime.

This is what the reporters see, while they hear the prisoner charged with breaking and entering, assault with a deadly weapon, burglary, indecent exposure, attempted rape, murder, or any of the thousands of crimes in the statute books.

The job of the reporters is to report the arrest. But they would like to do more. Their stories will make juicier reading if they can mention a confession, stronger still if they can cite *details* of the confession. The police, too, would like to do more. If they cannot prevent a crime, they would like to solve it. They will try to get that confession. If they do, they are further likely to tell the reporters. They might even leak a few *details*. It makes good publicity for the force, a good story for the reporter. Reporters print these things, knowing that what they print could damage the prisoner's right to a fair trial; that, in fact, many confessions are inadmissible as evidence in a trial; that many times the suspect hasn't even had the chance to consult a lawyer.

Reporters also include other background information. They find out if the prisoner has a record. They locate his relatives. They find out where he works, the name of his employer, how many children he has, their names, and where they go to school. They find out who his friends are, and whether or not any of them has ever been in trouble with the law. They find out everything they can for inclusion in follow-up stories.

In October, 1964, a New York *Times* reporter reported the

arrest of six suspects in a narcotics case. The headline read:. DAUGHTER OF OIL EXECUTIVE IS SEIZED IN BROOKLYN. The only consequence of this headline is to embarrass the father of the girl, to make him guilty by association. In the body of the story, the reporter identified the father by name, pointed out that he was "aviation manager for the —————— Oil Company," and gave his home address.

Describing the other suspects, the reporter listed them in this fashion:

B——— D———, 22 a laborer . . . who has a burglary conviction; B——— S———, 23 . . . a salesman with convictions for assault and robbery, forgery, and illegal possession of a weapon . . . [The above names have been withheld by the author.]

All this information shows admirable conscientiousness on the part of the reporter. He did a thorough job. In doing it he gave prejudicial information which might later have been ruled completely inadmissible in court. Jurors who know of prior convictions might easily become biased by that knowledge; indeed, that is why such evidence is usually not admitted. Judge Irving Kaufman granted a change of venue because just such information was published. A reporter fulfills his function if he simply reports: "John Smith was arrested last night, in Trenton, New Jersey, on suspicion of burglary. Patrolman Brown was the arresting officer." This may be colorless. It will not fire the imagination of his editor, and certainly it won't bring readers flocking to the newsstands. But surely, it will give John Smith a better chance for a fair trial.

A perfect example of the kind of temptation to which reporters often succumb occurred in October, 1964. The crime was nonviolent, but so romantic that it attracted nationwide press attention. The largest star sapphire in the world—the Star of India, a priceless, incomparably beautiful gem—was stolen from its glass-enclosed case at the Museum of Natural History in New York City.

As it happened, one of the great motion-picture successes in New York at that time was a film called *Topkapi*. *Topkapi* was about jewel thieves who broke into a museum and almost got away with jewelry valued at about the amount of the U.S. national debt. The similarity was astonishing. (Perhaps Congress should investigate the effect of movies, rather than television, on our crime and delinquency rate.)

The crime itself was committed in mid-week. Within hours there were dozens of theories about "how" the robbers did it. The most popular theory, of course, paralleled the movie: the robbers had let themselves in from the roof, dangling precariously, head down, at the end of a rope, waiting—sweat dripping *up* their faces—for the guards to pass, while the gem glowed and beckoned only inches away. Seventy-two hours and three arrests later, the New York police and the FBI announced that they had cracked the case. Thunderous headlines and excited TV commentators blared to the nation the news that the case was solved.

In point of fact, no case is solved until the suspect has been found guilty by a jury of his peers. Until that moment, theoretically, the case is wide open and the person on trial is innocent. If the jury brings in a verdict of innocent, the police must go back to work.

The facts were that the FBI had arrested three men suspected of stealing the jewels. No one saw the jewels; no one saw the men at the museum. There were reports that fingerprints were found all over the museum case from which the jewels were taken. Fingerprints in a museum are not the most conclusive evidence in the world. How many people might have looked through that glass case at those gems—and even pointed, fingers resting on the glass, at the wondrous two-and-a-half-inch sapphire?

Reporters covering the story burst forth with evidence that should have been released only in a courtroom. Television reporters arranged an interview with the police officer in charge of the case. He said, to an audience of millions—and he obviously did not have a doubt in his mind—"They just know too much about it to be innocent." This is close to a standard phrase with police officers on television. Their suspects always know too much about the crime to be innocent.

Reporters Nora Ephron and Gene Grove covered the great museum robbery for the New York *Post*. The front page of the *Post* (a tabloid) was all headline: HOW GEM THEFT WAS BROKEN. WILD PARTIES LED TO TIP, GIRL FRIEND LED TO ARRESTS.

The story itself began:

The three men charged with the Museum of Natural History jewel robbery entrapped themselves in a mesh of mistakes which, the New York *Post* learned today, led to their arrest. The three:

Engaged in a three month long round of wild parties and reckless spending which drew attention to them.

Let a casual acquaintance know that they carried huge wads of money, owned a jeweler's scale, were interested in gems, and visited the Museum of Natural History every day.

Frightened a girl friend of one of the alleged thieves by inviting her to Miami, then forcing her to fly south under an alias and carrying a locked briefcase.

The story goes on to say:

During the days, they would drive to the Museum of Natural History and amble through. They sat on the benches outside, they took pictures of the approaches to the building, they photographed its room from the roof of a nearby building, they photographed the gems in their cases, they bought books and floor plans in the museum store.

Thursday night *the FBI says* [italics here and below added], Clark stood guard while Murphy and Kuhn, dressed in dark clothes, sneakers, and gloves, executed the acrobatic theft which involved lowering themselves on a nylon venetian blind cord into the fourth floor hall housing the J. P. Morgan gem collection. They took 24 jewels, including what Clark later referred to as "The Big Three—the Star of India sapphire, the Star Ruby, and the Midnight Sapphire."

Still further in the same story:

Miami Beach Detective Chief Arthur Leonard said, "All three are crack jewel thieves. They're topnotchers and we've been trying to pin something on them for a long time. . . ."

Clark has admitted, *police say,* acting as a lookout but says Kuhn and Murphy were the ringleaders and he does not know where the jewels are. He was held in $12,000 bond on charges of burglary, possession of burglary tools, possession of marijuana, and violation of the Sullivan Law.

After reading this, and seeing Kuhn, Murphy, and Clark file into a courtroom under guard to begin their trial, what would a juror feel about their guilt or innocence?

But that story appeared in one of the "popular tabloid" newspapers. On that score, possibly, it might be discounted by the juror.

On November 2, 1964, the New York *Times* reported:

The police in the Bahamas had several contacts with two of the suspects earlier this year.

The first was several weeks after a $750,000 jewel theft in Nassau. A yacht with the two suspects and three other men aboard turned up at Bimini and was searched by the police there. Nothing was found.

Nine days later the yacht appeared at the island of Andros. While the yacht was in Andros, there was a jewel robbery at a hotel there.

Officials found no evidence of crime on the yacht, but the men aboard were turned out of Bahama Islands' waters and told not to return.

The *Times* reporter also mentions the narcotics charges against Mr. Clark, re-creates the details of the robbery, and points out that photographs of the roof and interior of the museum were found in the New York apartment rented by the suspects.

The *Times* considers itself, and is considered by others—with justification—a leader in the fight to preserve civil liberties. Yet reading the *Times* story is enough to make most people think, "Those prisoners have got to be guilty."

On the graph of responsible journalism, the New York *Journal-American* falls between the *Times* and the *Post*. The *Journal-American* quoted a Miami detective:

The three had been under surveillance for six weeks before they came to New York. . . . "It was not an around the clock thing. We just wanted to be aware when they were in our area and when they left.

"There had been many jewel robberies while they were down here and people like that are always suspect."

Miami police officers disclosed [author's italics] that Kuhn was known to carry sums as high as $20,000 as pocket money.

The reporter for the New York *World-Telegram & Sun* filled his story with references to a $550-per-month suite in a New York hotel, and a $287-per-month apartment in Florida.

He also quoted police as reporting that Kuhn and Murphy had gotten in by opening a locked door with a celluloid strip.

The New York *Herald Tribune* man wrote:

Although the New York police are saying not a word, it is reliably reported [by whom?] that the lone member of the alleged robbery trio picked up here—Roger Clark of 68 Willis Avenue, Meriden, Connecticut—is telling the police a mouthful about the jewel robbery.

Mr. Clark's mother, absolutely uninvolved in the robbery, got undeserved mention in all the stories.

There are six major New York daily newspapers, the *Times, Tribune, News, Post, Journal,* and *World-Telegram.* Their combined circulation approximates 3,250,000 per day. It would be safe to estimate readership at double that figure. At the least, more than 6,500,000 people read the "evidence" that these men were the jewel thieves.

The men were to be tried in New York City, whose population stands around 8,000,000. Thus, almost seven of every eight people in New York read the stories. Perhaps every adult read them, since the 8,000,000 population figure includes children. Where would the city find a juror unfamiliar with the crime, unbiased in his feelings about the defendants? Every one of the six newspapers ran a damaging story. A literate New Yorker could not have avoided reading about the case. Even those who, somehow, might have missed the newspaper stories were blanketed by radio and television.

The accused men might have been guilty, but under our Constitution they were innocent on the day those stories ran. Under our Constitution, perhaps, but in the view of their peers? Undoubtedly not.

Most of the stories included references to statements made

by the FBI, the New York police, and the Miami police. Certainly these stories make the police look good. Certainly they indicate that the police are on the job, that they move quickly and surely. Police are not immune to the pleasures of favorable publicity. They get enough undeserved bad publicity. That they should want to be seen in a good light is understandable. The police, for the most part, do an excellent job. But catching *suspected* criminals is their job. Supplying the press with information is not. It is up to a jury to make criminals of the suspects. If, by the information they give, the police create the danger of an innocent man's being convicted and jailed, the police have failed in their mission.

As it turned out, the great museum robbery didn't get to a jury. The suspects confessed. But the finale to the story remains a direct refutation of the press's protestations that it does what it does always in the public interest. Of paramount importance to the public was the return of the gems to the museum, so that their beauty would again be available to visitors.

That the return of the gems was the primary concern of the law authorities was evidenced by the willingness of the authorities to offer light sentences to the defendants, if the defendants returned the gems.

The defendants agreed. At that point one of them, Allen Kuhn, with several detectives, tried, secretly, to fly from New York to Miami, where the gems were hidden. Secrecy was important. Publicity could frighten off others, in Miami, whose cooperation—in return for secrecy and immunity to prosecution—was needed to recover the jewelry.

Secrecy was not to be. The press got wind of the trip, descended on Kuhn and the detectives, and all but destroyed the chances of recovery.

The New York *Times* reported that, when the newsmen

discovered the whereabouts of the group in Miami, "Evasive maneuvering began, most of it to avoid the reporters and photographers, *some of them hiding in bushes, some carrying walkie-talkies and some pulling ignition wires on cars the authorities had rented so they would not start.*" [italics added]

At one point the detectives even had to jump *thirty* feet from their motel window to the ground to keep a secret appointment. They could not leave through the front door because of the hordes of newsmen.

Despite the harassment, the detectives managed to accomplish their mission. They recovered most of the gems and returned to New York. Newsmen learned of the return, and were present in such numbers when the group got to their own offices in New York that two of the detectives had to force a path through the crowd. Asking for help from the newsmen was futile. One detective finally had to shove so hard that he knocked over three cameramen and a huge television camera. That is how the press works in the public interest when there is a crime story to report.

These men turned out to be guilty. Yet neither the press nor anyone else knew that when the case broke in the newspapers. They might have been innocent. Their punishment, in any case, was only a jail sentence. But what if the crime involved could send an innocent man to the gallows, the gas chamber, or the electric chair because reporters did their job overwell?

In October, 1964, a reporter for the New York *Times* wrote this story:

TWO BOYS, 12, FACE
SLAYING HEARING

They Will Be Arraigned in Brooklyn Court Today

Two twelve-year-old boys will be arraigned today in Brooklyn

Children's Court as juvenile delinquents, charged with robbing and slaying a seventy-two-year-old woman on September 28 in the twenty-room mansion where she worked as a housekeeper. The youngsters were arrested Saturday night *after they had accompanied detectives to the three-story house at 457 Clinton Avenue where they re-enacted the crime* [italics here and below added].

They are alleged to have confessed that they entered the house shortly before dawn and went to the top floor where they said they strangled Miss Louise Schultz in her bed. They allegedly took $20 from her, then went to the adjoining bedroom where they beat Miss Delia Walsh, the maid, and robbed her of $2.03 which was in her suitcase. Miss Walsh had described her attackers as a Negro youth, the police said. [*sic*]

The two youngsters have long histories as problem children. They had been classmates at Public School 613 at 387 State Street, Brooklyn, one of the "600" schools for disturbed and maladjusted children.

In addition, one of them had been in and out of Creedmore State Hospital at Queens Village for mental treatment for about a year.

The Creedmore records listed the child as a schizophrenic. Authorities there said he had fled from the institution last July 30 while being visited by his father. He was reportedly returned to Creedmore on September 29. Hospital officials said the youngster was "a nice boy with a warm personality and an uncontrollable desire to steal."

Detectives John Flynn and Richard Byrnes picked him up Saturday night near his home for questioning in connection with an investigation of theft from patients at the Brooklyn Eye and Ear Hospital, which is near the Clinton Avenue mansion. *His home is in an adjoining area.*

The detectives said that while questioning him at the station-house *he confessed to the murder* and involved the other 12-year-old boy as an accomplice. *They said that during subsequent questioning both boys told them facts about the murder that the police had not released for publication.*

The two were in custody last night at the Youth House in Manhattan.

Anyone who reads this story must finish convinced that the two boys are guilty. If they were not guilty, how could they have re-enacted the crime? That they did re-enact it is evidence that should be introduced only in trial, when jurors can hear it for the first time; not in a newspaper, when people who might become jurors can read it, and ponder it, long before they are ever selected to sit on the jury.

Why must readers know, before trial, that the two children have long histories as problem children, that they attended special schools set aside for disturbed children? Why must they know, before trial, that one of them was a patient at a mental hospital, that he was classified as schizophrenic, that he had once escaped the hospital, that he had an "uncontrollable desire to steal"?

The impression (or worse, the certainty) left with a reader is that these boys have all the qualifications for committing murder—that indeed they did commit murder.

Finally, the *Times* reporter printed that old standby of police officers who make public statements about a suspect— that the suspects told them facts about the murder and robbery that only the perpetrator could know.

It would be in defiance of all the laws of human nature if a reader could finish such a story and say to himself, "Perhaps they are innocent after all." The net result of that story is the practical impossibility of finding a fair and impartial jury to try the accused boys.

The day after the above story appeared in the New York *Times*, the following story was printed:

PROSECUTOR BACKS
BOY'S CONFESSION

Says He Feels Statement on Slaying Is Reliable

Aaron Koota, Acting Kings County District Attorney defended yesterday the truth and reliability of the confessions
of two twelve-year-old boys to the murder of a seventy-two-
year-old woman.

*One of the boys appeared to have a perfect alibi when
authorities at Kings County Hospital stated on Monday that
he was a patient in a locked psychiatric ward at the time of
the slaying.* . . . [italics added here and below]

In a statement yesterday, Mr. Koota said: "I have arrived
at a conclusion with reasonable certainty as to the truth and
realiability of these statements [the confessions]. In view of
the fact that proceedings involving the two boys are now
pending in the Family Court, I will make no further comment."

*Informed sources said,** however, that after investigation
the District Attorney was satisfied that the boy, who had a
history of escapes and attempted escapes from mental institutions, had slipped out of the ward by unlocking the door with
a bent spoon and had returned after the killing in the same
day.* . . .

According to the physician, hospital bed check records established the boy had been in the locked ward throughout the
three days.

On Tuesday the *Times* reporter virtually condemned two
boys to conviction. On Wednesday he all but established their
innocence.

Certainly the boy who had been locked up in a mental
hospital was just as innocent on Tuesday as he was on
Wednesday, even though the "why" of his innocence had not
been discovered. In actual fact, both boys were innocent. But

* See Chapter 3, The Unpluggable Dike.

even if they had not been, they should have been presumed innocent until a jury foreman intoned: "We find the defendants guilty."

Yet suppose the alibi did not exist. Suppose he had not been locked up in a mental hospital, but instead had gone to a movie, alone, or had taken a long walk, alone, or had remained home watching television, alone. He would have been no less innocent. But could he have found "twelve good men and true" who would have believed him innocent?

The dilemma of the reporter was articulated best by a reporter—Jimmy Breslin, of the New York *Herald Tribune*.

A man named Mark Fein had been indicted for the murder of a bookie. The police charged that Fein, a wealthy man, owed huge gambling debts to the bookie and that, rather than pay them, he had killed the bookie.

While the trial was in progress, Breslin wrote a column—a very moving column—describing his interview, just outside the courtroom, with the dead man's brother.

Finally the give and take of the courtroom was over and the jury retired to deliberate. At that point, Breslin journeyed to the courtroom to gather material for one final story on the case. There he encountered the families of Mark Fein and of the murdered man. He wrote about them, about the courtroom itself, about the detectives in the case, and about some of his own thoughts. His story appeared in *New York* magazine, a supplement to the *Herald Tribune*.

In part, his story reads:

This is what all this talk about press coverage of criminal trials comes down to. The defense lawyers say that stories about a man's crime influence juries and innocent people go to jail because of it. New Jersey has just put together a rule forbidding lawyers, police and prosecutors from talking to newspapers before the trial is finished. Then an associate dean from a law school says he has confidence in the wisdom of a free press. The Warren Commission Report differed and said the press needs a code to govern itself in the handling of crime stories. England, they keep saying, the English system is best. Nothing is allowed to be printed before a trial. When they arrest a man in England, the papers say, "John Jones is helping Scotland Yard into the inquiries of the murder of Ann Smith."

Protect the innocent. Whatever you do, protect the innocent. A man is innocent until proven guilty. Mark Fein, right now, is innocent until this jury comes in. He was innocent when you wrote the column quoting Reuben Markowitz's [the slain man] brother as saying he was guilty. If somebody on the jury read the column, they [sic] might be swayed and if Mark Fein were innocent they would vote him guilty.

It's all proper and impossible to argue against when you put it on paper and cite rules and theories. But then you go out, with four hours to do a job, and a body has been found in a river and a man has been arrested by the police and indicted by a grand jury and what do you do? You report it and you report everything else that happens in connection with the case and if they put a rule in about this, then they can put in a rule about something else and then you can have this great English system. . . .

And when you work at newspapers for a living, with only so much time in a day, all these arguments come down to the light [of hate in Mark Fein's father's] eyes and I look at them and say the hell with it, I was just doing a job.

There are some jobs, after all, too well done. And done so well only at the expense of others.

SIX

The Zealousness Transplant: Newspapers to TV

IF IT WERE POSSIBLE to measure the impact of a specific story on an audience, an x impact on newspaper readers would inevitably be worth about 5x on a television audience. One is all too familiar with the newspaper story describing a young, mustached, sallow, pimple-faced youth weighing about 214 pounds, wearing tight black pants and a black leather jacket, sneering defiance and jests at the police who accuse him of a crime, as they lead him (handcuffed) into headquarters. One reads this, and then forgets the description five minutes later. But star this same youth on television, in the same scene, and the man is long remembered by those who see him. Let him "look" guilty, on camera, and his troubles increase. If he is Negro, or obviously a member of another minority group, he is in still more trouble. The precise degree of trouble is probably in proportion to the number of people who see the telecast, multiplied by the number of times he appears on the air. These are the people from among whom a jury will be selected.

Television does not make a deliberate effort to prejudice its viewers. It is simply that TV is more powerful than any other medium of communication. What we see on television remains with us. (If it did not, television would not be so powerful an advertising medium.)

Seeing is believing. It is that simple. (TV could restore organized religion to the power status it once enjoyed if licenses were granted by churches instead of by government. If that were the case one could predict that public-service broadcasts would be religion-oriented instead of government-oriented as they presently are. Bishops instead of politicians would *Meet the Press* and *Face the Nation*. Religion would enjoy a new renaissance.)

Whether it wants it or not, TV holds power: almost ultimate power. In at least one area—the reporting of crime news —it could exercise this power more responsibly. Indeed television frequently exhibits less than a humane sense of responsibility toward the rights of a criminal suspect.

With the millions it makes in profits, television has bought itself a magnificent collection of newsmen: reporters, writers, photographers, commentators, and weather girls. It has supplied them with the best equipment. Their microphones can pick up a sigh at hundreds of feet, their cameras are mobile enough to intrude on the privacy of dozens of people in an hour, their film can record pictures in near darkness, and their new, relatively portable videotape recorders turn out show material in a fraction of a second.

Television newscasts have forced the construction of a complete TV studio in the White House, made presidential press conferences a camera-hogging holiday.

Nowhere has this revolution been quite so marked as it has been in police coverage. Television stations, particularly in the larger cities, have what amounts to their own prowl cars outfitted with radios tuned in to police- and fire-department frequencies. Let a hint come over those frequencies about a crime, an arrest, or a fight, and TV's reporters and cameramen converge on the spot within minutes.

If the TV men are lucky, they get to headquarters in time to snatch from the prisoner the first of the many rights he will ultimately lose: his right of privacy. They poke their microphones into his face, their cameras into his path, and let loose with an avalanche of questions (and they are always the same questions, no matter what the crime or who the prisoner). "Did you do it?" "Why did you do it?" "How do you feel?" "Does your family know about it?" "Did you have any accomplices?" and so on. If a jury were present court might as well be held then and there.

TV's reporters corner the lawyers, the district attorneys, the policemen, the detectives, relatives, friends, and bondsmen. Everyone is fair game when the eleven o'clock newscast needs to be filled.

If the prisoner is lucky, he will not get out on bail. He will be kept in jail so he will not have to run that gantlet again. But TV men don't go home even if they cannot see the prisoner again. They look for a police officer who has talked to him.

We have all seen a camera turned loose on a studio audience. When that happens every arm within camera range starts waving like a tulip in a tornado. It is the only screen test most people ever get. It mustn't be wasted. The lens has the same effect on many policemen. Put one in front of a camera or a microphone and he is likely to become the most loquacious man in town. He knows many answers, and is all too willing to tell them to the world. What he tells is usually at the expense of the prisoner he has just booked.

The police tell where the prisoner was picked up, what crime he was booked for, the reasons for suspecting him in the first place, the additional evidence already gathered, his "absurd" denials of everything despite "ironclad proof" that he committed the crime. And, classically, the officer will finish with, "And he told us things that only the guilty man would know." All this on camera, almost in person, to the thousands or millions from among whom the jury will come. It is as if he were already a witness in the courtroom. It is worse, in fact, since on camera there is no defense attorney to cross-examine, to contradict him, to point out that much of what the officer says is hearsay, and therefore inadmissible as evidence. Everything the policeman says goes into the minds of the listeners unencumbered by argument from the other side.

In the long and unpleasant history of trial by press, the infant television provided the classic example of a suspect being condemned by the press. We all saw Lee Oswald tried before our eyes in a spectacular display of television's news-getting ability. We saw an even more disgusting display of news-giving by Dallas law-enforcement officials.

We know how Oswald fared with the Warren Commission. We shall never know, of course, how he would have fared before a jury. But we can guess that Oswald would not have had a chance.

There is a little-known case, however, *Rideau v. Louisiana,* which did get to a jury. This case, again, illustrates the insurmountable dangers of unbridled television coverage.

Just after the close of an ordinary business day, in Lake Charles, Louisiana, a business neighbor knocked on the locked door of the Southgate Branch of the Gulf National Bank. The people still working inside looked up when they heard the knock, recognized the knocker as a man they all knew, a man who worked nearby.

Without fear of any consequences, they opened the door and let him in. Julia Ferguson, Dora McCain, and Jay Hickman, the three employees still in the bank, knew the man well. They saw him almost daily in the course of their work.

But this time he was a changed man. He drew a gun, and at pistol point forced them to fill a suitcase full of cash. Since all four were well known to anyone who might be in the vicinity, the robber, without fear of discovery, ordered them out of the bank and into Julia Ferguson's car with the suitcase.

Still at gun point, he forced them to drive out of town to a desolate, uninhabited spot northeast of the town. By the time they arrived, the three must have guessed that they were the witnesses who would have to be destroyed to ensure the robber's escape.

They were ordered out of the car, lined up abreast of each other, and shot. Six shots, at point-blank range.

Jay Hickman, only slightly wounded, ran off. The (now) killer was not able to follow him immediately. He was too busy stabbing Julia Ferguson to death. His shots hadn't killed her. When she tried to rise to her feet, he realized that she was still alive so he stabbed her until no doubt was left.

Hickman, meanwhile, had fallen into a bayou. Assuming that all three were dead, the killer left with the suitcase full of money.

Hickman was not dead. He managed to reach the office of an oil company, and to tell the authorities the horrible story. Several hours later the police caught Wilbert Rideau and threw him into jail as a suspect. By this time the townspeople had learned about the crime, the shooting and the stabbing. They were, simply, bound for vengeance.

While news of the crime was racing through town, the police had Rideau in jail, where they were trying to get a confession from him. They must have been successful, and proud of their success, for the next morning camera equipment was set up in the jail. A local television station was about to make a movie. The stars: Rideau, the sheriff, and two state troopers. The plot: the story of the crime. Cameras, lights, and microphones were turned on. The stage was set and the plot unfolded.

There was Rideau, sitting in his jail cell flanked by two state troopers. Sitting with Rideau was the sheriff, asking questions about the crime. The sheriff asked leading questions, the prisoner responded. Rideau answered everything in detail. On camera, before he had seen a lawyer, Rideau confessed to the atrocities of the night before.

The filmed confession was broadcast in Lake Charles at least three times during the three days following the crime. Lake Charles parish (county) has a population of 153,000. Reliable audience estimates put the size of the combined audience watching those three telecasts at about 106,000 people. Allowing for minors not eligible to serve on a jury, this would indicate that nearly every adult in the parish had seen the film at least once. Those who didn't see it must have heard about it.

Yet the judge in the case could not bring himself to believe that seeing the film might prejudice the minds of potential jurors. When Rideau's lawyers filed for a change of venue (to hold the trial somewhere else, where public indignation—or knowledge—could not play a part in the jury's decision), their motion was denied. Rideau was forced to stand trial in the town where his confession had been broadcast to virtually everyone.

Rideau pleaded innocent by reason of insanity. He was convicted and sentenced to death.

There were many embarrassing questions in the case. First, why did Rideau not have a lawyer as late as the morning after his capture? (Why didn't the TV men ask that question?) Certainly enough time had passed for the court to assign one to him. No good lawyer would have permitted him to stage a confession for benefit of television. Second, why did the sheriff go along with the urgings of the TV people for a filmed interview? Third, who had the idea for an interview to begin with? Fourth, what kind of management did that television station have, that it would allow that interview on the air? Fifth, what kind of legal counsel did the station have? Any lawyer with a sense of justice must have known that so inflammatory an interview, broadcast to the entire population of the area, must deprive the defendant of due process of law.

The Supreme Court upset Rideau's conviction, saying that the motion for a change of venue should have been granted. It further said that the forum for Rideau's trial was not the courtroom, as it should have been, but the television set.

At this writing, Rideau is awaiting a new trial, in a new place. (There have been many appeals to the Supreme Court on the same grounds, and often the court has not only sustained the original verdict, but has even refused to hear argument.)

Rideau could have been executed. Yet suppose he actually was insane when he committed the murders. The filmed interview would make it more difficult for a jury to believe that this was the case. Or suppose, after the appeal, Rideau had been freed. The town of Lake Charles would have become an armed camp with every door and window locked, children escorted to and from school, a gun in the hand of every store-keeper.

By its actions in the Rideau case, television certainly gave the best picture of the news, but that picture also made "due process of law" impossible of achievement. Television served no one: not itself, not Rideau, and certainly not the people it is licensed to serve "in the public interest."

Radio, too, is able to take a suspect and make a convicted criminal of him. The case of the *Baltimore Radio Show v. State of Maryland* bears witness.

Rule 904 of the Rules of the Supreme Bench of Baltimore City was, in pertinent part, as follows:

In connection with any case which may be pending in the Criminal Court of Baltimore, or in connection with any person charged with crime and in the custody of the Police. . . . whether before or after indictment, any of the following acts shall be subject to punishment as contempt:

*   *   *

C. The issuance by the police authorities, the State's Attorney, counsel for the defense, or any other person having official connection with the case, of any statement relative to the conduct of the accused, or other matters bearing upon the issues to be tried.

*   *   *

E. The publication of any matter which may prevent a fair trial, improperly influence the court or the jury, or tend in any manner to interfere with the administration of justice.

*   *   *

F. The publication of any matter obtained as a result of violation of this rule.

On the early afternoon of July 6, 1948, in Baltimore, Maryland, Marsha Brill, an eleven-year-old girl, was stabbed to death by an unidentified man while she was at play with two other children. Public indignation was at once inflamed.

At about 10:45 P.M. on the same day, Eugene H. James was arrested and held for investigation. On the afternoon of July 8, 1948, he was taken to the scene of the crime, where he made an oral statement to the police admitting his guilt, and directed the police to the spot where he had buried the murder knife. At about 6 P.M., James was formally charged with murder at the Northern Police Station. A few hours later James signed a written confession.

About 7 P.M., a Miss Taggert, night editor of the United Press, called Hamilton R. Atkinson, police commissioner of Baltimore City, stating that she intended to write a story embodying the information he would either give or verify for her. Commissioner Atkinson verified some of her information and supplemented it. Later that evening he was interviewed by the press outside his office at police headquarters and, in response to questions, gave further information, although he denied that he gave a formal press release for publication.

At 9:45 P.M. Miss Taggert's story was dispatched by United Press teletype. This dispatch was received by three local radio stations and broadcast at various times in slightly different forms. The three radio stations were The Baltimore Broadcasting Corporation, WCBM; Baltimore Radio Show, Inc., WFBR; and Maryland Broadcasting Co., WITH. The broadcasts, which varied only slightly from station to station, were, in most pertinent parts, as follows:

Stand by for a sensation!

After three days of unrelenting hard work on the part of every man in the department, the Baltimore police have just broken the Brill murder case—broken it wide open. Police Commissioner Hamilton R. Atkinson announced only a few moments ago that a man had been arrested and formally charged with the crime—the brutal and apparently pointless stabbing of eleven-year-old Marsha Brill in the Pimlico neighborhood Tuesday afternoon. The funeral of the little murder victim was held today and hundreds of persons attended. The man now charged with the Brill girl's murder is Eugene James, a thirty-one-year-old *Negro and convicted former offender* [italics added here and below], whose home is . . . not far from the scene of the crime.

The police said James not only admitted the Brill murder and another recent assault in the same area but that he went over the scene of the crime with them late this afternoon and showed them where the murder weapon was buried. It turned out to be an old kitchen carving knife. Immediately after the finding of the knife the prisoner was taken downtown to police headquarters for a formal statement. The story of how James came to be charged with the Brill murder is an account of police work at its best. *James was taken into custody yesterday mainly because of his record. Police remembered that he had been charged or suspected in past years with a series of assaults and that about ten years ago he was sentenced to the Maryland penitentiary for an attack on a ten-year-old child* . . .

James was questioned, along with other suspects, but no information of much importance was obtained from him until today. The police did not use any force, of course, but questioned him persistently. Then, this morning, *according to the officers, James admitted* an attack on a white woman recently in the same woods near where the Brill girl was slain. In that case too, James used a knife, but only to threaten his victim into submission. She was not otherwise injured. With more information supplied by James, police recovered the woman's pocketbook, which he had taken from her. *Police said* James was familiar with every foot of the ground on which the offenses, the assault of the woman and the slaying of the girl, occurred. James is not an obvious mental case. Throughout all his questioning, said the police, he seemed, as they put it, "quite cute," in other words, wary. When James freely admitted the assault on the woman the police were encouraged and renewed their interrogation with renewed vigor. They felt that James had admitted the lesser assault only to throw police off the main track, and the police felt they were close to a confession in the Brill case. They were in fact.

A few hours later the prisoner broke again and this time it was the break that broke the Brill case. James admitted that crime also and consented to accompany the police to the scene. On the ground, said the police, he made a more detailed confession. . . .

The first hint that the police were close to an important break in the Brill case came *with word from an officer of rank at headquarters* that, while no arrests had yet been made and no charges had been placed, the police felt they had a very good suspect. At that time, he had not confessed the Brill crime, although he had admitted the earlier offense against the woman in the same neighborhood. . . .

The police are deserving of the utmost commendation for the comparatively quick break in the case, and the commendation is merited by every man who worked on the assignment from the highest to the lowest. From the first Commissioner Atkinson personally took charge of the investigation. The hunt for the slayer promised to be a long, hard routine search. The killer had escaped from the scene despite a wide dragnet thrown around it soon after the alarm. Usually when an arrest is not made on or near the scene such cases develop into long, exhausting investigations that end, usually, only when the police get some favorable break. In this case, the officers made their own break by remembering James' record and taking him in hand promptly. Had the police not been so alert and so prompt James might have fled the city. With the prisoner in hand, all the rest was accomplished by patient and skilled interrogation. Dozens of suspects were examined and released until the police felt reasonably sure that the lone man remaining in custody was the one they wanted.

The police are to be congratulated. And it is tragic that all

the community can do otherwise is commiserate with the
bereaved family. . . .

And now a brief pause. Here is our announcer, Gil Kriegel,
again with a message from our sponsor. I'll be with you again
in a moment with more news and comments. . . .

On July 9, 1948, James was indicted by the grand jury of
Baltimore for the Brill murder, and for the assault and rape of
a certain white woman some weeks before the Brill murder.
At his arraignment, James pleaded, through his counsel, not
guilty and not guilty by reason of insanity. On September 20,
1948, James was tried for murder. His counsel waived a jury
trial because, as he later explained, he "felt that, inasmuch as
it was common knowledge throughout the city that James
had, allegedly, made a confession and that he had been previously convicted for a crime somewhat similar to his then
present indictment, I [his attorney] did not feel that I could
have picked a jury that had not been infected, so to speak, by
the knowledge of this man's confession and his criminal background." James was found guilty and sentenced to death. The
court under the rules quoted above cited the three radio stations for contempt of court. The Maryland Court of Appeals
reversed the citation under rule 904-E because it interfered
with freedom of speech; thus 904-E was unconstitutional.

Some, or at least one, of broadcasting's higher executives
has finally recognized the enormity of the problem of broadcast coverage of crime news. Dr. Frank Stanton, president of
CBS, in several forthright speeches made clear that he knows
that television can insinuate itself ineradicably into the minds
of men. He has admitted publicly that TV newscasts can
make it difficult if not impossible for a suspect to get a fair
trial.

Thus far, despite Dr. Stanton's plea, there have been no

new industry-wide standards drawn up to govern the reporting of such news—much talk but no action, and crime coverage on television continues as before.

Unless it pays heed to constructive suggestions such as Dr. Stanton's, television will do more to make fair trials impossible than newspapers have been able to do in a hundred years.

SEVEN

Who Speaks to the Grand Jury?

IN MOST STATES, and in the federal jurisdiction, no suspect can be brought to trial unless he is first indicted by a grand jury. The grand jury, usually a body of twenty or more people, hears evidence presented by the district attorney's office and then decides, by majority vote, whether or not there is sufficient evidence to charge the suspect with a crime. Grand juries exist, theoretically, to protect people suspected of committing a crime from the powers of vengeful law-enforcement officers. Only civilians sit on grand juries; it is their function to prevent an unfair indictment and to insist on an indictment when a district attorney seems too lenient.

Theoretically, too, grand jurors are selected with greater care than are members of petit (trial) juries, since they represent the all-important first step in the administration of justice. They must be as objective as humans can be: free from partiality and preconceived notions, able to separate fact from emotion, willing to free a man who merely looks like a criminal or to indict a man who happens to look innocent.

The action taken by a grand jury becomes overwhelmingly important when it is remembered that indictments make big news, and that in many ways an indictment is as damaging as a conviction. Too many of us proceed on the basis of "where there's smoke, there's fire." When we read that a person has been indicted, some of us have an automatic tendency to conclude that he is guilty. We don't stop to consider that an indictment is no more than an *accusation*, a way for the district attorney to say to the courts: "We think this person is guilty; we think we have enough evidence to convict him of a crime; we intend to bring him to trial."

When a person is indicted he is often severely ostracized by his neighbors, by his friends, and, unfortunately, by his employer. It is difficult for him to make the community believe that, at the conclusion of his trial, there might be a verdict of "innocent."

Thus the effects on grand jurors of unrestrained crime reporting can, conceivably, be the greatest evil of this entire problem. If grand jurors, under the influence of sensational newspaper stories, vote to indict, they start a process terribly difficult to bring to a halt short of total disgrace to the indictee.

We have seen this very situation in a preceding chapter. Earl Warren, then a district attorney in California, used the press to prod grand jurors into voting indictments against public officials and private citizens in a graft and construction scandal, by releasing to the press the testimony given to that grand jury.

At once, Warren exhibited the two facets of the problem. He used the press to influence grand jurors, and he used the grand jury's evidence as fodder for newspaer stories which did the defendants no good when they came to trial.

The Johnny Dio case, mentioned earlier in connection with "leaks" to the press, illustrates yet another instance of gratui-

tous information about a suspect being published prior to the
deliberations of a grand jury. In 1956, the New York *Times*
carried the following story:

JOHNNY DIO AND 4 OTHERS HELD AS
MASTERMINDS IN RIESEL ATTACK

Johnny Dioguardi, alias Johnny Dio, *considered to be*
[italics added here and below] one of the most powerful
labor racketeers in the nation, was accused last night of having arranged the acid attack that took the sight of Victor
Riesel. . . .

Dio, *a convicted labor extortioner . . . was said to have
arranged for the attack on Mr. Riesel with Charles Tusco, a
garment worker with a police record dating to 1931.*

He [Dio] *has served time in Sing Sing Prison for extort-
ing funds from truck owners and manufacturers in the garment district* in the thirties. Since then he has been active in
teamster and garment labor affairs. District Attorney Hogan
last month branded him *"one of the most powerful underworld figures"* in labor. Two years ago *he was convicted of violating the New York State tax laws, and last June he was
indicted for conspiracy and bribery in a plot to exact $30,000
from an electroplating company as the price for labor peace.*

This story appeared in similar detail in the rest of the New
York press.

People chosen as grand jurors are, by design, more aware
than the average citizen of the world and the events in it. It is
impossible to believe, then, that some, if not all, members of
the grand jury considering Dio's case had not read these stories. No matter how objective a grand juror is supposed to be,
how will he react, listening to testimony about Dio and remembering at the same time that he read that Dio was convicted of at least two other crimes, serving time in jail at least
once?

As a matter of fact, Dio's lawyers had moved that the indictment be dropped on the ground that the grand jury *had* been influenced by newspaper stories.

The court denied the motion, but nonetheless wrote in its opinion:

It does appear from newspaper accounts that there were detailed statements by representatives of the United States Department of Justice made even before an indictment was filed in this case, to the effect that the crime had been "solved," and setting forth in detail the persons by whom and the manner and means by which it was committed. . . .

To the extent that "trial by newspaper" was indulged in by Federal law-enforcement officials, it is to be regretted and condemned . . .

[The court is not] willing to suppose, assume, or conjecture, as a matter of fact, that the grand jury deliberations were so infected as to invalidate the indictment; although it must be added, in all fairness, that *such a supposition would do little violence either to the conscience or the imagination.* [italics added]

If Dio had been on trial, evidence of past indictments and convictions would have been inadmissible unless he himself had taken the stand. There can be no references in court to the prior criminal record of a defendant unless that defendant chooses to become a witness in his own defense. This kind of evidence is inadmissible precisely because it can influence a juror against the defendant, even though it has absolutely nothing to do with the crime that brought the defendant to court.

It seems odd and unfair that what the law has found prejudicial is permissible in newspapers. Mr. Dio was indicted by the grand jury, convicted in court, and went to jail.

Shortly after it printed the story above, the New York *Times* editorialized about this very case:

CONVICTION BEFORE TRIAL

The tendency of some lawyers and prosecuting attorneys to try their cases in the newspapers bobs up now and then, with potentially harmful effects on the course of justice.

The latest example of what is, in substance, a "trial by newspaper" [italics added here and below] is to be found in statements released to the press of this city last week by Federal law-enforcement authorities on developments growing out of the acid-throwing attack on the labor commentator, Victor Riesel. Arrests have been made, accompanied by sensational statements from the F.B.I. and the United States Attorney's office—*statements that clearly implicate or even convict the accused of despicable crimes before they have been indicted, much less tried in the courts.* . . .

The press itself has a responsibility to treat with restraint pre-trial information, whether handed out by police, prosecutor or attorneys. But the press cannot be expected to refrain from printing statements issued by public officials, as for example the United States Attorney, even though such statements may be prejudicial to a fair trial. . . . The only way to stop this abuse is to stop it at the source. . . .

Again, an admission of interference with justice joined with a refusal to acknowledge that the interferer can do anything about it. And again, the prisoner suffers.

Johnny Dio was guilty. There is no doubt of that. It is probably accurate to say that, in the cases cited, most of the defendants found guilty were guilty. Yet remember Airman Anderson (Chapter Three) who could have been found guilty of a murder someone else committed. There may be others like him.

There are those who feel "Who cares how they were put in jail, so long as they get there? We can't have people like *that* running around loose. If an innocent man goes to jail, that's the price we pay for protection against the guilty." But our

concern must be the one man who might be sent to jail—after
the publication of prejudicial newspaper stories—*even though
he is innocent*, a fact he may never be able to prove.

It is unfortunate, but true, that we do not become aroused
about newspaper excesses as long as the guilty are punished.
This failing on our part does not condone the unjust activities
of the press. How must we feel when we read in the New York
Times that "harsh competition" prevents the press from carrying out its "responsibility to treat with restraint pre-trial information"?

I have a friend who serves on a grand jury in a medium-
sized community on Long Island, New York. I asked her,
"What effect do newspaper stories about a crime or a suspect
have on you when you're sitting as a grand juror? Do they
influence you at all? Are you able to ignore them when you
are trying to reach a decision?"

She replied, "Well, I say this to myself: 'The police
wouldn't have him there at all if he hadn't done something
wrong.' " My friend the grand juror presumes the suspect
(who is not yet even a defendant) guilty only because the
police have brought him in, even before he has spoken a
word. She never did reply to the original question, but it
would seem credible that, feeling as she does, she does not
attempt to discount newspaper and television stories.

It is too much to hope that grand jurors pay no attention to
what they see in the press. Perhaps there are a scant few who
have that facility, but can we ever be sure?

Grand jury deliberations are supposed to be secret to protect the interests of the suspect not only if he is not indicted,
but also if he is. News of grand jury testimony could prejudice
chances for a fair trial. It would seem only logical that this
secrecy would apply, too, to the comings and goings of wit-

nesses before a grand jury, particularly since appearances before a grand jury are looked upon with raised eyebrows. (Try to convince a next-door neighbor that you are not implicated after he has learned that you were questioned in the X affair.)

Yet in any case of importance the press seems always to know when to have its reporters and photographers stationed at the entrance through which witnesses must pass. Is it too much to hope that editors, knowing that these activities are secret, would not assign reporters to them? In this instance the press cannot even plead, legitimately, that it must print what the authorities disclose. It knows that the authorities have no right to disclose anything.

A perfect example of the press reporting comings and goings to grand jury rooms occurred during the TV quiz investigations in New York City in 1958 and 1959.

It is true that, while the deliberations of the jury were not leaked to the press, some of the testimony was (perhaps by some of the witnesses themselves, rather than by Mr. Hogan's office). Nonetheless, whenever a contestant of national renown was scheduled to appear, stories about him, with photographs, would find their way into the New York press following his appearance. During the early, sensational days of the investigation, Charles Van Doren seldom escaped the camera's eye.

The press was told, too, when certain potential witnesses refused to waive immunity. And these stories, of course, appeared in the newspapers.

A witness before a grand jury, at least in New York City, can refuse to answer questions put to him on the ground that he might incriminate himself. If he does refuse, the grand jury can grant him immunity from prosecution and then direct him to answer. When that happens he must reply to questions, although he can do so without fear of self-incrimination.

However, if a prospective witness is someone the district attorney may want to prosecute, he may ask the witness to sign a waiver of immunity. If the witness signs he must testify and thereby, possibly, incriminate himself. Usually if the witness has something to fear he will refuse to sign the waiver. When this happens the district attorney, knowing that the witness's testimony cannot be too productive of truth, generally dismisses him.

Unfortunately, a refusal to sign the waiver of immunity too often winds up as a newspaper story the next day. There can be only one inference drawn from a story saying, "John Doe refused to sign a waiver of immunity." In the mind of the reader John Doe has something to hide; he is guilty of something or he would have signed. This sequence, too, happened to several figures involved in the quiz investigation.

In 1964 it happened again, this time to many members of the New York City police force. A full-fledged gambling scandal broke on the city during the spring and summer of that year. Everywhere one read that members of the police force had been bribed to look the other way when bookies were making book.

The revelations shook the city, as had similar charges ten years earlier. Newspapers ran editorials calling for a "clean-up." Grand juries were impaneled to take testimony.

The district attorney's office ordered a parade of witnesses to the grand jury room. Many testified. Several others, including some high-ranking police officers, were asked to sign waivers of immunity before they testified. Of these, a good number refused to sign. When a member of the police force of

New York City refuses to sign a waiver, suspension from active duty is an automatic penalty.

These officers were suspended. Newspapers carried the stories of their refusal to sign the waivers, and of their suspensions. It would be safe to predict that not many New Yorkers (including the author) presumed these officers to be innocent of wrongdoing.

Yet, had we not read that they had refused to sign we would have formed no conclusions. That is as it should be. Or should have been.

Another example of unwarranted publicity concerning the actions of a grand jury was the scandal that exploded within the State Liquor Authority of New York. This scandal had been brewing (not a pun) for years before a disgruntled licensee decided not to remain silent any longer. He went to District Attorney Frank Hogan and his staff, and the repercussions reached the upper echelons of the New York State Republican party. The allegations were that no one could obtain a liquor license, or even transfer one to a new location, without paying huge bribes. Nearly everyone was supposed to be in on the take—from lowly field investigators to those at the very top.

The chairman of the State Liquor Authority was Martin Epstein. He was ordered to testify before the grand jury. Ill-health (he had had a leg amputated, and several heart attacks) caused a postponement of his appearance. His wife was subpoenaed to testify. She refused, even after receiving immunity, and was cited for contempt. Authority employees by the score scurried in and out of the grand jury room. At least one suicide was attributed by the police to the investigation.

New Yorkers read it all in their newspapers, saw it all on

their television sets. They knew who had testified and who was supposed to testify. Reporters cornered witnesses on their way out and did their best to worm out of them the supposedly secret details of what transpired within the grand jury room.

Long before the grand jury finished its deliberations there could not have been a New Yorker who, having heard the stories, did not believe that the State Liquor Authority was thoroughly corrupt. As it turned out, these suspicions—the very worst of them—were confirmed. The graft and bribery were almost too much to comprehend. But the public should not have learned, when it did, about the individuals involved. Not only did this knowledge make fair trials difficult, it probably gave many of those involved in the actual chicanery a chance to cover their tracks before the investigation got to them.

In his investigation of the famed Museum of Natural History jewel robbery in November 1964, the district attorney of New York had the grand jury question many witnesses— guards at the museum, officials, jewelry experts, and so on. None, or almost none, of the innocent witnesses got their names into the newspapers. But a young girl who had supposedly befriended the alleged jewel thieves made the papers when she testified to that same grand jury. This is the story that appeared in the New York *World-Telegram & Sun*:

GIRL IN GEM
THEFT PROBE
TALKS TO JURY

An attractive brunette, whom police described as the unwitting courier in last Thursday's gem theft from the Museum of Natural History, testified briefly before a grand jury today.

But the witness, Janet Florkiewicz, 19, refused to speak to newsmen as she scurried from the grand jury room. Miss Florkiewicz wore dark glasses and kept her head down.

In addition to Miss Florkiewicz, who is being held in protective custody in lieu of $5,000 bail, the grand jury heard several witnesses in its investigation of the $410,000 jewel theft. . . .

Why was Miss Florkiewicz singled out? Doesn't there remain, after reading the story, a feeling that she could not be entirely innocent?

Of all the institutions designed to safeguard the individual against harsh and unfair treatment from his government's law enforcers, the grand jury is the most important. It is the individual's first line of defense. Surely, in this area at least, we have a right to hope that even those portions of the press that resort to sensationalism will live up to their responsibilities.

EIGHT

The Fiction of Responsibility:
Part-time Press Cooperation

IT IS POSSIBLE under the law to cite a newspaper for contempt when a news story interferes with "due process of law." This procedure is seldom used. Instead, authorities use the weak alternative of "requesting" the press to refrain from printing stories that might be prejudicial to a defendant. This is, at bottom, nothing more than an appeal to better instincts, with no recourse, no penalty, if the appeal is ignored.

This process of "requesting" cooperation seems a strange luxury. We do not "request" that people avoid criminal activity; we send them to jail if they don't. We do not "request" honesty in school examinations; students flunk, or worse, if they are caught. We would not have an atomic-test ban today if we had not developed almost infallible methods of detecting a breach of the ban. We do not have disarmament because we cannot find, with Russia, a mutually accepted and enforceable system of inspection.

In short, we do next to nothing on faith. Yet on faith we ask the American press to refrain from publishing information potentially prejudicial to a defendant in a criminal case.

It is time to recognize that the entire press does not keep the faith, that its erring members have erred often enough to demonstrate the need for legislative restraints on all the press.

In 1935 the presiding judge in the Lindbergh kidnaping trial, in deference to the press and the legal right of a defendant to a "public" trial, permitted the installation of a camera and sound equipment in the courtroom. The judge also ordered, quite explicitly, that no pictures were to be taken while he was on the bench. Despite the judge's request, the cameraman muffled the camera equipment in a soundproof hood, installed remote-control equipment, and had the camera in operation while some of the most important witnesses testified. When you make a deal with the human factor, you deal in probabilities.

This story, unfortunately, is not the exception to the rule, though there have been instances of press cooperation. The problem is that there is no way to predict with any accuracy when the press will heed a request to cooperate and when it will ignore it.

In most instances of press cooperation we find that the request originated with the court or an officer of the law rather than as an initiative of the press or its representatives. In all the investigation undertaken for this book we found nothing to indicate that a newspaper has ever said to a court or to a district attorney, not to speak of its own public, "It would be unfair of us to print this." Of course, this does not mean that examples of cooperation are unwelcome. It does mean that we cannot rely on the press to provide self-improvement.

In 1937, in Cleveland, Ohio, the state, attempting to get a grand-jury indictment against two so-called labor racketeers, had great difficulty persuading witnesses to testify at the grand jury hearings. The potential witnesses were, at worst, frightened of possible reprisals against them and/or their families and, at least, anxious to avoid publicity. (See Chapter Seven, Who Speaks to the Grand Jury?)

The prosecutor called the press in and asked that it neither print the names of the witnesses nor photograph them. The press having consented, the prosecutor informed the prospective witnesses that they would not be publicized in any way. The witnesses testified. On the basis of their testimony the grand jury returned an indictment.

Then the problem repeated itself. Now that the two men were indicted they would have to stand trial. To win a guilty verdict at trial would require the same witnesses to repeat their testimony in open court. Publicity at that point would have been just as dangerous or unpleasant as it would have been during the grand-jury hearings; indeed, the results could have been worse. The prosecutor knew that the witnesses, again faced with the probability of publicity and its attendant dangers, would be under strong temptation to "forget" the testimony they had given to the grand jury, or even to perjure themselves.

Again he went to the newspapers and asked them not to photograph the witnesses in court. The press agreed, and again the witnesses testified without fear of reprisals.

It seemed to be an era of good feeling, of relative cooperation between press and courts. In 1938, New Jersey had to prosecute two girls, both under twenty-one, for the murder of a bus driver. Public interest in the case began to rival the Lindbergh case. The prospects for cooperation were faint; the press had come on strong when the suspects were caught. William Barhorst, a thirty-four-year-old bus driver, had been shot to death on December 21 of the previous year. His murderer stole Barhorst's change carrier containing $12, but dropped most of the money in the hurry to get away. The getaway was in a stolen car driven by an accomplice. It was a $2 killing.

On January 4, 1938, police caught two suspects. On January 5, the New York *Times* headlined its story this way (all italics added):

TWO GIRLS ADMIT $2
HOLD-UP KILLING

Newark Policeman's Daughter, 20, and Friend, 17, *Confess* in Bus Driver Slaying

Met in Reform School

Laid Plans There for Crime Career
Police Say—Linked to Another
Robbery

In fewer than forty words that headline announced a confession and a past criminal record, and disclosed that the girls planned a career of crime. Possibly none of this would have been admissible in court. Certainly it had not yet been presented to a grand jury.

There was not much reason to hope that the press would cover the trial any differently from the way it covered the arrests.

Judge Brennan, the trial judge, realized the enormous publicity potential of the trial, however, and he was determined to avoid it. Prior to the opening of the trial he called in three reporters, one from each of the three local newspapers. He asked them to find out how many reporters the wire services and the New York papers intended to assign to the trial, and what kind of coverage they planned. The three reporters learned that a minimum of twenty-five reporters would cover the case and would be in court daily.

The judge called all of them in for a meeting. He told them that no messengers would be allowed in the courtroom to pick up their copy, that instead the court would provide two attendants to whom the reporters could hand their stories. He told them that he would allow no photographs to be taken in the courtroom while he was on the bench. He polled the jurors, who indicated very strongly that they did not wish to be photographed at all. The defendants, through their attorneys, agreed to allow one photograph of themselves, to be taken when the court was not in session.

With the one seemingly inevitable exception of a photographer who tried to take pictures secretly, all the agreements were respected. That photographer was banished from the trial.

The two girls were convicted of first-degree murder, with a recommendation of mercy. They could have received the death penalty. They were sentenced to life imprisonment.

It might seem that, with the trial about to get under way, the judge was being unduly cautious, or alarmist, in his quest for responsible, nonsensational coverage of the proceedings. After all, jurors are instructed not to read newspaper accounts of a trial, not to listen to TV or radio coverage, and not to discuss it. In Dallas, Texas, jurors are locked up from the moment a trial begins until they reach a verdict. But jurors in New Jersey, as in most other places, are not locked up until all evidence has been taken and it is time for them to deliberate. They go home each night, and despite all warnings and exhortations to the contrary, surely must come into contact with the communications media. (They have ample opportunity to read about a case before they are even selected to serve on the jury.) Even if they cannot (or should not) read the newspapers, their families go on doing so. And even if they are cautioned not to discuss the case with anyone, they cannot control inadvertent remarks by a member of their family—remarks possibly based on a news story. If the case is getting significant attention, that possibility becomes even stronger.

Judge Brennan, then, was doing everything he could to provide due process of law for the two young defendants when he "imposed" cooperation on the press. And it was "imposed."

After the trial the Newark *Sunday Call* (no longer in existence) editorialized:

The Sohl-Owens trial which attracted wide attention throughout the country demonstrated that sensational criminal cases can be conducted with decency and dignity without much difficulty. All that is needed is a firm judge and lawyers who are mindful of their professional obligations. Newspapers and the public take their cue from the Bench and Bar. Judge Brennan directed the trial with wisdom and justice.

Again we find that the press is unwilling to regulate itself —"Newspapers and the public take their cue from the Bench and Bar."

It is true. We cannot rely on the press to regulate itself. In Akron, Ohio, in 1959, a judge ordered that "no photographs are to be taken while the court is in session." The then chief photographer of the Akron *Beacon Journal* took a picture, while the court was in session, through a glass window on a door leading into the courtroom. He knew of the judge's restriction when he took the photograph. The judge fined him $100 for contempt of court, explaining that his restriction obviously meant "No photographs were to be taken of these proceedings."

The photographer appealed. His contempt citation was reversed on the ground that the judge's order had stated that no pictures were to be taken in the courtroom and that he had taken *his* while outside.

Certainly that was the letter of the law. But the photographer, as a representative of the press, with equal certainty violated its spirit. In doing so he demonstrated all too strongly why many leading jurists today insist that there will never be voluntary cooperation from the press in its coverage of crime stories.

The most discouraging aspect of many of these instances of press failure to cooperate with the courts is that so frequently it appears to be not a failure at all, but a deliberate flouting. Certainly that is the only way to characterize what happened in the case of *United States v. Powell*, in 1959.

The defendants were charged with conspiracy to violate the draft act. During the trial the government prosecutor wanted to introduce evidence that the defendants published a magazine called the *Chinese Monthly Review*. He also wanted to introduce other evidence pertaining to the behavior of the defendants during the Korean War.

Pending his ruling on the admissibility of the evidence, the judge dismissed the jury but allowed the press to stay while he heard argument from the prosecution and the defense. He decided that the evidence was not admissible. He further said that had the defendants been charged with treason the evidence would have been admissible, since rules of evidence in treason cases are broader. The jury returned and the trial continued without hearing that portion of the prosecution's evidence.

The very next day two San Francisco newspapers carried

banner headlines proclaiming that the judge had declared the
"Powells guilty of treason," and that the judge "flayed the
Powells."

The defense immediately moved for a mistrial. The prosecution agreed that the jury probably was prejudiced by those
headlines, and the stories that appeared under them. The
court granted the motion.

The court, in ordering the mistrial, added:

Courts, particularly in criminal cases, are zealous in protecting the rights of a defendant against the possibility of the
jury being influenced by non-evidentiary matters. Consequently, it has been traditional to excuse the jury, and to keep
from their ears arguments on legal matters such as the admission of evidence. This we did in this case. Nevertheless, the
press, in disregard of the worthy purpose above stated, published and disseminated that which the court had kept from
the ears of the jury. . . . "The doctrine of freedom of the press
is not for the benefit of the press, but for the benefit of the
people."

The press, in arguing that its freedom must not be limited,
uses the same contention advanced above by the court—that
freedom of the press is for the benefit of the people, that the
people have a right to know. Obviously, this is construed by
the press to mean that it can decide *what* the public has a right
to know.

Two facts are clear. First, the reporters, by receiving permission to remain in the courtroom even though the jury was
asked to leave, knew that they were about to hear evidence
that the judge did not want the jury to hear. Even if they did
not at that moment understand what was happening, it was
made unmistakable when the judge decided that the evidence
was inadmissible. Despite this, the two San Francisco newspapers deliberately published the story. Even more important

was the agreement by prosecution, defense, and the court that the jury was probably prejudiced by the newspaper articles. This clearly signifies that all three parties realized that the jurors, or some of them, must have read the articles.

Remember, though, that jurors are told by the judge at the beginning of a trial not to read newspaper or magazine accounts of the trial, not to listen to television reports of the trial, and not to discuss the case with anyone. The Powell case indicates that prosecutors, defense attorney, and magistrates are not too confident that jurors heed the rules of the court; jurors, despite warnings, undoubtedly do read newspapers while a case is still in progress. Beyond that, it indicates that interested parties accept the fact that newspaper stories influence jurors. And above all, it means that no one—not the court, not the defense, not the prosecution—has any real faith in a juror's ability to put aside what he has read or heard and to reach an objective decision based solely on what has been revealed in the courtroom.

In this light, one hopes that our federal and state legislatures will some day define what the public has a "right to know" in terms of crime news. Further, one must hope that these same legislatures will make cooperation something more than voluntary.

If there is any doubt remaining about the need for strict legal definitions of cooperation, it must be dispelled by the Weinberger kidnaping case in New York City.

The Weinberger baby was one month old. On the hot afternoon of July 4, 1956, his mother put him in his baby carriage in the back yard of their home in Westbury, Long Island. When she next went out she found, instead of her baby, a ransom note demanding $2,000. The note threatened that the infant would be killed if the police were notified, and left instructions as to where the ransom money should be left. The indicated place was not far from the Weinberger home.

The Weinbergers did notify the police, who, because of the kidnaper's threat to kill the baby, asked total secrecy of everyone, including the press. They especially did not want the kidnaper to know that the spot he had designated as the drop for the ransom money was known to them. They hoped to save the child and capture the kidnaper at the same time.

Early on that evening of July 4, the July 5 edition of the New York *Daily News* hit the newsstands of New York City and suburbs. (The *News* comes out earlier than any of its competitors. It is always available the evening before the date indicated on its masthead.) Its front page carried this story:

MONTH OLD L. I. BABY KIDNAPED

A four-week-old boy was kidnaped from his carriage on the porch of his wealthy parents' home in Westbury, Long Island about 3 P.M. yesterday, and a ransom note, demanding $2,000, was left by the snatcher. . . .

Nassau County police, respecting the wishes of the father, Morris Weinberger . . . threw a curtain of secrecy over the case.

The same day, in a later edition, the *News* described the place where the kidnaper had instructed the parents to leave the money:

The note gave instructions for leaving the money at a specified garage in the neighborhood.

The New York *Daily News* was, at that moment, the only newspaper in New York City to carry the story. All the other newspapers had respected the request of the Nassau County police to withhold publication of the story.

As soon as the public read the story telling where the money was to be dropped, hundreds of reporters and the just curious raced to the spot. The ransom money was there but the kidnaper, frightened and probably furious, made no attempt to pick it up. He left, and abandoned the month-old baby in a wooded area not far from its home. The infant died of exposure.

After the *News* broke the story, the police released the other newspapers from their pledges of secrecy, and they all printed it. The damage had been done; it was both unfair and pointless to expect the rest of the press to withhold publication any longer.

Inspector Stuyvesant Pinnell, chief of the Nassau County detectives, enraged by the "story *über alles*" attitude of the *News*, stormed at reporters: "We would have gotten a hell of a lot further if there had been no interference from the press and you can quote me on that." That same day the baby's mother said to the press, "I could cut all your throats."

The *News* denied that it published the story in spite of Inspector Pinnell's request for secrecy. Robert G. Shand, managing editor of the *News*, maintained that he had received an early tip on the case, that the story had been printed and on the streets forty-five minutes before Pinnell made his request. By the time Pinnell spoke up, said the *News*, it was too late.

It was curious, though, that the New York *Mirror*, which got to newsstands only moments after the *News*, did not run the story. Nor did the New York *Herald Tribune* or the New York *Times*, which are also on sale at about the same time. It is probable that the *News* did receive an advance tip about the story. Yet any editor or experienced crime reporter also knows that newspaper stories of kidnaping can mean the death of the kidnaped child.

The New York *Times*, which does not wantonly attack its competitors in print, editorialized:

It is the business of a newspaper to report the news. Sometimes, however, a newspaper finds it the necessary or at least the humane thing to do to stop and ask whether a given story should be reported, and when, and whether a life may be put in jeopardy by premature publication of all or certain details. We regret that one New York newspaper apparently failed to do so. Other papers were ready to honor the request of Nassau County police that the story of the kidnaping be temporarily withheld, the morning after the little boy was taken from his carriage, until the ransom directions were followed.

The baby's kidnaper, a twenty-one-year-old mechanic, was caught. He told the police that the baby was still alive when he went to pick up the ransom money.

Some time later Inspector Pinnell said, "It is not our purpose to fight with the press or any segment of the press. But we are not going to be charged with the death of a child whose life we did everything to save while the real responsibility rests elsewhere."

The inspector said, too, that he had personally telephoned the newspaper (he never identified the *News* by name) to ask its cooperation. He produced telephone toll bills to substantiate his statement. In response to his call, Pinnell said, the newspaper "notified me that, *despite an urgent plea from its Nassau reporter* [italics here and below added], it was going ahead anyway and print the full story.

"I asked, 'Isn't a human life worth more to you than a story?' The answer was, '*I agree, but* I was told to call you to tell you that *we can't hold the story.*'"

Pinnell then added, "Somebody had made a fateful decision, utterly destroying our efforts at secrecy, the secrecy needed to help us get back the baby unharmed. I would not want such a decision on my conscience."

By being the only newspaper to print the kidnaping story, that night of July 4, the *News* might have picked up a few thousand extra readers—for that one night. But there isn't a scale in the world that balances additional readers against a human life.

NINE

Objective Reporter, Subjective Report

W E DECIDE for ourselves only what we wish to say. The inferences drawn from our words by others are outside our control. Not only are we rich in synonyms (or what people think are synonyms), most of us are not careful enough, or informed enough, to select words bearing the precise meaning we wish to give.

The imprecise definition of words, moreover, is not confined to things we ourselves write. It is equally prevalent in the way we define, in our minds, the words used by others. If we read about a "big" man, one reader will imagine a fat man while another will imagine a tall man.

There are flocks of girls who swear they heard marriage proposals, and legions of boys who claim they proposed no such thing; hordes of authors are misinterpreted by hosts of critics.

Even more dangerous than the misuse and misinterpretation of words, though, is the tendency of eyewitnesses to a specific act to see or hear entirely different things.

The Civil Aeronautics Board has great difficulty with this whenever it investigates an airplane crash. Witnesses testify that the plane was a thousand feet high and five thousand feet high; that the engines seemed to be making funny noises and that the engines seemed to be operating smoothly; that the plane was in a steep turn and that the plane was heading nose first toward the ground; that there was a loud explosion before the plane hit the ground and that there wasn't a sound before it hit the ground.

Reporters, though trained to be better witnesses than ordinary mortals, are subject to these same failings. Reporters, even if less often than others, nevertheless use words inaccurately, interpret words inaccurately, and witness events inaccurately.

But we rely for our information on newspaper stories written by reporters. We believe what we read in the newspapers.

This situation is bad enough if it is only a football game or a political speech being reported. If the story concerns a crime, the consequence to the defendant might be injustice—constitutionally rendered. (The danger would not be as great, would perhaps be nonexistent, if the story were to appear after the trial.)

No trial in years was more heavily publicized than that of Jack Ruby. On trial for killing the alleged assassin of President Kennedy, his trial corralled reporters from everywhere in the world. They converged on Texas to supply their readers with every detail they could lay their hands on. Shortly after the trial ended, Dallas' District Attorney Henry Wade told me, "The only really accurate reporting to come out of this trial, the only reporters who really seemed interested in checking their facts after the daily sessions in court, came from the New York *Times*. Even the *Times*' stories had mistakes, but not nearly as many as the other papers I read." Mr. Wade added that he obviously hadn't had time to read more than a tiny segment of the press, that he didn't intend, by his statement, to impugn all the world's newspapers. He said enough, though, to make one wonder how much faith to have in the accuracy of the newspaper coverage.

Life magazine assigned Sybille Bedford to cover the trial. Miss Bedford, even before that assignment, had acquired a reputation as a crime specialist. She had covered some of the more extraordinary English murder trials, and had written a book on a notorious French murder case; there was no reason to question her credentials.

After the trial her long, excitingly written account of it appeared in *Life*. No reader, certainly not this reader, would have had much difficulty discovering that Miss Bedford found fault with the jury's decision. Though *Life* published it as a news story, with pictures, it was far from that. It was her *opinion* of the facts presented at the trial.

A week after it appeared Melvin Belli, Jack Ruby's attorney, referred to Miss Bedford's article as "the only accurate reporting to come out of the whole trial." The next day District Attorney Wade told me that 50 per cent of the facts in Miss Bedford's story were inaccurate. (Neither Mr. Belli nor Mr. Wade was totally accurate in his estimate of Miss Bedford. But comparison of the trial transcript with the *Life* story indicated that Mr. Wade had stronger grounds for his position than did Mr. Belli.)

To make matters worse, the reporter is only the first step of the long, complicated trail every news story must follow before it reaches the reader. On larger newspapers, a story goes from the reporter to a rewrite man. He touches it up, cuts it down to fit the space allotted to it, adds an adjective here, changes one there. Then the story goes to the copy desk, where grammatical corrections are made and the headline is written. The city desk is involved too. It must decide on which page to print the story and how long the story shall be.

Only after a story has gone through all these hands is it ready to be set in type and printed. Any of these people can, knowingly or otherwise, change the meaning of the story turned in by the reporter. Changes in meaning must, inevitably, creep into the finished story.

There is also the rewrite man who may purposely set out to give his work "style." There is no limit to what he can do to a story, if he wants to.

S. Burton Heath, a very famous and respected reporter for the New York *World-Telegram*, points out in his autobiography exactly how much of a danger a rewrite man can be:

While I was on rewrite, I was puzzled by the fact that whereas I always seemed to get rather routine stories, one of my fellows never failed to get each day at least one or two vivid human interest items, that read like pages from a novel. Reporters gave me the pertinent facts, but he always had intriguing dialogue and his stories usually had a fillip at the end. I rated as a competent rewrite man, but he was fast becoming a star.

In the course of time I was sent out on stories, and eventually I telephoned one to him to rewrite. When the edition came out I hunted for it in vain. At last, reading a most interesting little piece, I experienced that feeling one does, at times, of living through something that has happened before. With some difficulty I discovered the reason. The story I was reading was this chap's version of the very commonplace item I had telephoned to him. His fertile imagination had changed the facts beyond recognition. He had done no injustices, nor did his version deceive readers about anything important. It was just a triple-short story, based upon the news incident and run as news, without the editors' knowledge that it wasn't an accurate report.

(Heath points out that this happened while the newspaper was

still the New York *Telegram*, before it merged with the
World.) Heath's rewrite man was just one of thousands of
rewrite men. If he succumbed to the temptation to dress up
his story, can we suppose that he was the only man in the
nation ever to succumb? Beyond that, can we accept Heath's
disclaimer that "he had done no injustices, nor did his version
deceive readers about anything important"? Who decides for
me the way I interpret facts, the meanings I read into
them?

In 1960, this headline appeared in a Chicago newspaper:
THERE'S A CAPONE ECHO AT ACCARDO TRIAL.

The story under the headline read: "In the villain's part this
time was Chicago's jet-age Capone—stony-faced . . . Accardo, the master of muscling legitimate business."

One cannot say that the reporter who found a comparison
between Capone and Accardo did it maliciously, hoping to
impassion the minds of the jurors. Yet, because of the words
the reporter used, he gave the clear impression that he thought
Accardo was consciously trying to be another Capone.

Accardo, convicted at that trial, had his conviction reversed on appeal. The appeals court found prejudicial publicity.

Then there are reporters who forget that a news story is
supposed to report only facts, not opinion. None other than
Alexander Woollcott, a writer greatly lauded for his use of the
English language, when he was reporting the trial of Bruno
Richard Hauptmann wrote:

Yet if there is one thing crystal clear in this curious and
intricate case, it is that the young man [Hauptmann] to
whom the designated go-between handed over the $50,000

was either the kidnaper himself or one so privy to the crime at its very inception as to be black with guilt from head to toe.

Woollcott did not qualify his story by saying that it was "crystal clear" to *him*. By that omission any reader might easily have inferred that Woollcott's statement was itself the truth, that it had been demonstrated in court and accepted by the jury that Hauptmann was guilty.

Much more recently (October 6, 1964), the New York *World-Telegram & Sun* printed this headline across the top of page one:

D.A. ASSERTS MORHOUSE ASKED $100,000 BRIBE

The man referred to in the headline was L. Judson Morhouse, prominent lawyer and former state chairman of New York's Republican party. His name automatically meant big news. The story went on to say:

Former Republican State Chairman L. Judson Morhouse demanded $100,000 from Playboy Club officials to get them a liquor license, Assistant District Attorney Jeremiah McKenna said in Supreme Court today.

McKenna told prospective jurors at the bribery conspiracy trial of Ralph Berger, a Chicago public relations man, that the $100,000 was to be paid over a five year span. . . .

Morhouse last year refused to waive immunity before the grand jury investigating corruption in the State Liquor Authority.

The story was written by one Erwin Savelson (who probably did not write the headline). At any rate Morhouse (when the story appeared) had not been indicted for bribery. He was not on trial. The money he allegedly demanded could have been nothing more than a legal fee. The story could have used the word "fee," and allowed a future jury, if any, to decide if it were a "bribe." In the body of the story reporter

Savelson, by using the phrase "at the bribery conspiracy trial
of Ralph Berger," included the unmistakable implication that
Morhouse, too, was part of that conspiracy. Yet Berger was
on trial not for trying to bribe Morhouse, but for participating
in a conspiracy to pay a bribe to the then chairman of the
Liquor Authority.

Perhaps there was no intent to damage Morhouse. Whatever the intent, he was damaged.

On the same day that the New York *Daily News* was running its account of the Berger trial, and mentioning Morhouse
just as prominently, it carried (on the same page) the following:

KNIFE-KICK YOUTHS SLASH 3

By Edward Kirknan and Henry Lee

In a wild knifing, punching, kicking spree, three teenagers
viciously attacked a fellow student and, during the next hour
and a half . . . knifed and beat two men without provocation.

Though they demanded money, they seemed more interested in getting their senseless kicks. . . .

They denied any knowledge of the assaults.

The reporters used adjectives—"wild," "viciously," "senseless"—which had no place in the story; they were not needed
for accuracy, might indeed have been inaccurate. There is no
doubt of course, that any knifing, kicking, or punching is a
"wild" act, any attack is a "vicious" attack. Since we are
aware of that, it is not news. Then there is the use of the word
"spree," with its connotation of joy, or pleasure. This is a
word of attitude. It would go harshly with the defendants if
the jurors came into court feeling, in advance, that the attacks
were part of a spree. The two reporters made a trial decidedly
dangerous, rather than a protection, for the defendants. They

did it *without* being inaccurate. Accuracy is not enough if the truth is varnished.

If such suspects were found guilty, their attorney could appeal their convictions, arguing that prejudicial publicity made a fair trial impossible. If the appeals court sustained the appeal it could mean freedom for the suspects. Yet suppose they had been the actual attackers. What, then, would the free press, in its protection of society's "right to know," have done for society?

On a June evening in 1964, eighteen-year-old Joan Wilson was returning to her home on West Forty-second Street, in New York City. Chatting with a friend, she suddenly crumpled to the ground, dead, a bullet through her forehead.

Five months later the police arrested a suspect. The New York *Herald Tribune* headline writer turned the arrest into a bonanza:

THE 42ND ST. SNIPER MYSTERY SOLVED [It wasn't solved. A suspect had been arrested.]

The reporter, Paul Weissman, opened his story with these paragraphs:

It was 1 o'clock in the morning last June 23rd when pretty little Margaret Wilson, 13, skipped happily down Eighth Avenue after the graduation party at Holy Cross Lyceum, 321 W. 43rd St.

Joan, her 18-year-old sister, was with her and they turned right at 42nd St., tired and happy after the party, unafraid of being alone after midnight. Home was only a block away at 420 W. 42nd St.

Joan Wilson never got there. She stopped to talk with a friend in a parking lot at 361 W. 42nd St., and there she died. A 38-caliber sniper's bullet struck her forehead and came out the back of her neck.

The rest of the story described the suspect, told how the police "solved" the murder.

Calculated or not, those paragraphs make you hate Joan Wilson's killer. Anyone arrested and identified by the police as the killer would be the target of that hatred, even before his version of the story was told, certainly before a jury had a chance to hear his story.

Weissman did not write a news story. He wrote a human interest story. He generated sympathy for the dead girl, sorrow for her family, and prejudice against the man accused of the killing. Yet, again, his story contained no inaccuracies, no half-truths, no innuendoes. Certainly Mr. Weissman did not intend to condemn the accused man. Unfortunately, effect seldom follows the path of intent.

A story reporting an arrest is no place for "good writing," for flavorful writing, for emotional writing. It is a place for facts. No more.

Contrast Weissman's story with the lead paragraph of the story that appeared in the New York *Times:*

A 25-year-old Marine sergeant was charged with homicide yesterday in the slaying last June of an 18-year-old girl in a Times Square parking lot.

That is enough. It tells the facts. It tells the public that a suspected murderer was captured, that a tragic crime might have been solved. It does it without recourse to sentimental adjectives, to emotional stimulus. What's more, it does it without mentioning the name of the suspect. (That happy circumstance did not prevail through the rest of the story—it went on to give the name, the evidence given out by the police against the suspect, and a quote from a detective saying the killing was "senseless.")

The degree to which subjective reporting can harm is illustrated by a story written by Tom Collins and Paul Meskil of the New York *World-Telegram & Sun,* on September 22, 1964. The story not very objectively tells of Anthony Spencer, arrested and accused by New York police of committing at least two rape-murders. It was headlined:

"HE'S SICK—AND I'M SO ASHAMED"

"I'm so ashamed," the woman said. "I'm ashamed to think I gave birth to a murderer."

Mrs. Rosalee Spencer, 43, sat in the living room of her Bronx apartment and spoke of her son, Anthony, "the only one of my six children who ever gave me any trouble."

But the troubles he gave her were nothing compared to the trouble he was in now.

According to police, the illiterate 17-year-old youth had confessed to sex murders and at least 10 rapes.

"He's sick," Mrs. Spencer said. "No normal person would do things like that. He is oversexy. When he was 12 years old I took him to Bellevue for psychiatric treatment. . . ."

"Only thing a judge can do is send him away to a hospital," she said. "If he's numb in the head and has to kill people, then he should be burned.

"The state can burn him up and can bury him too. I'm tired of looking in judges' faces. . . ."

When police picked him up for the first time, Anthony was only 11. He was accused of assaulting a 5-year-old girl. The child said he dragged her into a hallway, put his hand over her mouth and molested her, but she broke loose and ran away.

By choosing to report the story of Spencer's arrest in terms of his family—who were in no way connected with the crime —Spencer's rights were being sacrificed to flamboyant reporting. What bearing does a mother's bitterness have on a case? What kind of evidence is her defeated wail, "the state can burn him up"? What does a story like that contribute to journalism, to society, to justice?

The *Telegram* was not alone. Its story only set the fashion for reporting that arrest.

There appears to be no progress. Reporting of this sort was just as prevalent during the trial of Bruno Hauptmann for the kidnaping of Charles Lindbergh's baby.

The New York *Post* of January 29, 1935:

Hauptmann seems to me on the stand a thing lacking human characteristics, his face blotched, his mouth sagged, his eyes avoided all the other eyes that stared at him. He made senseless denials. He laughed pointlessly. I found myself thinking the creature must be insane, and then I began wondering if this too were not a carefully calculated pose, if, when a moment came when there was no answer, not even a senseless answer, which might stay the remorseless procession of Wilentz' [the prosecutor's] logic, Hauptmann would not leap and scream, and rave, posing as an out and out madman.

The New York *Mirror*, January 26, 1935:

A man who talks without tone, who sees without eyes, who whimpers without tears and who prays without hope, was Bruno Richard Hauptmann on the witness stand here today, as he told a story which he himself scarce seemed to believe will save him from the electric chair.

The New York *Mirror*, January 28, 1935:

Mark down this prediction. The name of Isidor Fisch, named by Bruno Hauptmann as the owner of the Lindbergh ransom money found in the Hauptmann garage, will positively be cleared before the noon session ends today in Justice Trenchard's Court.

The *Mirror's* reporter was so assured by one of the highest state officials who said:

Fisch will be eliminated as the possible writer of the ransom notes and therefore from having any connection with the crime. To his close friends, Prosecutor Wilentz has stated, "Fisch will not only be cleared of the accusation but it is likely that Hauptmann will admit it. The facts are impregnable and even the slightest defendant's stubbornness will melt under the barrage of truth."

Jack Lait, an "objective" reporter writing for the entire Hearst press: "I doubt anything could send a shudder through Bruno Richard Hauptmann except an electric current of high voltage."

To return to a case mentioned earlier in this chapter, the Anthony Joseph Accardo trial: there is a curious contradiction between some actual testimony, given in court, with the reporter's version of that testimony as it appeared in the next day's Chicago newspapers.

Accardo was on trial for allegedly giving false information in his income-tax return. (That is how the law caught up with Al Capone, hence the comparison—cited earlier—of Accardo with Capone.)

In court, Joseph Bronge, Jr., a government witness, testified that Accardo had worked for his father as a beer distributor, that Accardo had visited his home, that his (Bronge's) father was now dead, and that he (Bronge) had heard that Accardo was, at that point, distributing beer for himself. That was all of his testimony.

The next morning the Chicago press appeared with these headlines:

MURDER VICTIM'S SON TAKES STAND AGAINST ACCARDO
GANGSTER UPSET BY TESTIMONY BY BRONGE

The stories under these headlines, purporting to describe Bronge's testimony, said the same grand jury that indicted

Accardo had also indicted Bronge's father for perjury, that the father had subsequently been shot to death in a "beer war" because "hoodlums" were fearful that the elder Bronge would tell the police how he'd been forced to put them (the hoodlums) on his payroll.

Bronge, Jr., had not testified to any of that. Yet the newspaper accounts made it appear that he had. It is true that this information had appeared in one place or another. But by making it appear to have come from Bronge, Jr., the press also implied that Accardo was somehow involved in the shooting. Accardo was on trial for fraudulent statements on his tax return, but if the jury somehow connected him with the shooting and the gang wars it would be influenced in its decision in the tax case.

Apparently that is just what happened. Accardo was convicted. The appellate court reversed his conviction on the grounds of prejudicial publicity, *even though the jury denied violating the court's instructions against reading newspaper accounts of the trial.*

Obviously courts are not willing to believe that jurors really do not read newspaper stories of the trials they are involved in. And, equally obviously, the zealousness of a supposedly objective reporter negated an entire trial.

It is comforting to know that the men who report our news are well educated. It is not comforting when their knowledge appears in print in the guise of a news story. On November 16, 1960, in his story about a murder trial for the Pittsburgh *Post-Gazette*, a reporter wrote:

Although Assistant District Attorney Samuel Strauss indicated he would seek a second degree verdict because of the youth of the defendant, the testimony of two witnesses yesterday indicated that elements of the crime of first degree murder were present in the crime.

That reporter proved an old cliché. A little knowledge is a dangerous thing. The reporter had a little knowledge of the law. He paraded that knowledge in a news story. For a reporter to tell his readers, in a news story, that a defendant might have committed first-degree murder when officials are trying him only for second-degree murder, is to excite the passions of a community, to downgrade the efforts of the courts, and to be inhuman to one's fellow man. It is not being a reporter.

It is impossible to tell, at this time, whether what follows was the result of misinterpretation, or willful misrepresentation; whether it was a case of an objective reporter being subjective, or deliberately malicious. Whichever it was, it happened. It would seem a rather final argument for a change in our methods of handling crime news.

On April 27, 1962, the New York *Daily News* headlined a story: FATHER OF 4 ADMITS STRANGLING LOVE.

On the same day, writing about the same crime, the New York *Mirror* said: "He admitted he put his hand on her throat during a quarrel, but did not confess to killing her."

The first story qualifies a man for the electric chair. The second at least leaves room for reasonable doubt.

TEN

Pity the Poor Celebrity

PUBLICITY generated by the Errol Flynn case, when he was accused of the statutory rape of two girls, enriched our language by a phrase now in common use: "in like Flynn." One hears it from people who were not even born when that case was in the courts.

Flynn, found not guilty, was certainly convicted in the public mind. "In like Flynn" indicates nothing if not that the public believed he did what he was accused of doing. If the press had not treated the Flynn case as if it were a declaration of war, we would not be using that phrase today.

Miraculously, Errol Flynn was not convicted. This should not, however, give ammunition to those who say the press needs no restrictions. Errol Flynn had one of the greatest trial attorneys of California guiding his case, a lawyer who had never lost an important trial. Flynn could afford that lawyer. Few others could have. Whatever his fee, he was worth it. In the courtroom he was able to overcome the successful efforts of the press of the entire nation to characterize Errol Flynn as one of the great seducers of all time. Outside the courtroom, the characterization sticks to this day. Flynn, fortunately, was the kind of man who could carry it almost as a badge of honor.

Any story involving a nationally known celebrity or socialite is big news—and therefore a kind of hormonal stimulant to the instincts of all reporters. Any time a celebrity or a member of the social whirl is involved in a crime, a love affair, an accident, or almost any activity less commonplace than shopping at the supermarket, it becomes news.

Of course, by definition the celebrity needs to be in the public eye. He cannot be one without the other. No matter how much they deny it, celebrities enjoy seeing their names in print. There is no way of estimating how many millions of dollars celebrities pay each year to press agents to accomplish just this. The lack of privacy so many stars complain about is, at bottom, no one's fault but their own. It is not the intention here to make that fight for them.

When a celebrity is accused of a crime, however, it is another matter. Just as any ordinary individual, he wants no publicity at all. But that is when he gets more than ever.

Pre-trial publicity is more dangerous to a celebrity than it is to anyone else. The affections of the public are transitory, and within those affections there is a great deal of envy. Let a star be accused of a crime and that envy can turn, through our mysterious mental processes, into a certainty that the star is guilty.

Charlie Chaplin illustrates the point. He was involved in a paternity suit and a Mann Act charge at the same time.

Accused of fathering a baby, Chaplin had the mother of the (as yet unborn) child arrested for trespassing on his property. Chaplin maintained that he had had no kind of relationship with her for two years previously, but when she was arrested she told the police that he was the father of her unborn child.

The newspapers appeared immediately with stories blaring her accusation that Chaplin was the father of her child, that she was penniless, and that he, heartlessly, had her arrested because she came to his door to talk to him.

The paternity suit was brought in civil court, but the federal government secured a criminal indictment against Chaplin on charges of violating the Mann Act. Of his appearance in court for a preliminary hearing Chaplin said, "Press and photographers had a field day. They barged into the federal marshall's office over my protestations and photographed me while I was being fingerprinted.

" 'Have they a right to do this?' I asked.

" 'No,' said the marshal, 'but you can't control these fellows.' This was an official of the federal government talking."

To fight the suit, Chaplin submitted to a blood test. The test showed that the child did not have the same blood type as Chaplin's. Under California law today, that is positive proof that Chaplin could not have been the father.

Nonetheless, Chaplin was brought to trial in a civil suit charging that he was the father of the child. The first trial ended with a hung jury. The jury in the second trial decided that Chaplin, despite the blood test, was the father of the child.

The stories and headlines of the time appeared in huge quantities, and were uniformly nonobjective. Too, the case attracted as much newspaper space in New York, Florida, and Maine as it did in California.

Had the press anywhere in the country taken a man-in-the-street poll on Chaplin's guilt or innocence, as it so frequently does, there is little doubt that the man in the street would have found Chaplin guilty—again, only on the basis of what he had read in the press.

Who is prepared to say that the jury that found against Chaplin did not consider the "evidence" printed in newspapers, rather than the evidence of the blood test? How else could it have found that Chaplin was the father?

One needn't even be a star. Being related to a star is enough to win front-page space in a murder case. Suzanne Clift is the niece of Montgomery Clift. She was also a member of Boston society. The combination produced predictable results in the newspapers.

Following is a partial record of her treatment at the hands of the Boston and New York press during the five months preceding the disposition of her case.

On October 4, 1962, on page one, the Boston *Herald* headlined: ENGINEER FOUND SLAIN IN BEACON HILL MANSION. With the headline it printed a picture of Miss Clift, with the caption, "In Beacon Hill Mystery." The article went on:

The body was found shortly after Mrs. Pierce Pearmain, 71, Boston Society matron, returned at 4:30 P.M. to the house she owns at 85 Pinckney St. She had been away 10 days at her summer home in Oyster Harbors on Cape Cod. . . .

The room, *police said* [italics added], was the one usually occupied by her granddaughter, Miss Suzanne Clift, 21, a debutante of the 1958 season in Boston. . . .

Efforts to locate Miss Clift remained unsuccessful today. . . .

On the same day that the murder was committed, Commander Walter Schirra, Jr., became the first United States astronaut to orbit the earth six times. The Boston *Herald* felt that his story was big enough to share the front page with the murder story.

The next day, October 5, the *Herald* issued an "extra." The banner headline: DEB ADMITS KILLING ENGINEER.

The story read:

Suzanne Clift, blonde, 21-year-old socialite in whose bedroom the body of an Italian electronics expert was found Wednesday was under arrest for murder early today. . . .

[Boston Detective Lt. Edward] *Sherry later said the girl after questioning had admitted the shooting* [italics added] but would not give any reason for killing her boy friend.

A photograph, also on the front page, showed Suzanne Clift on her way to jail, escorted by detectives.

The page-one headline of the Boston *Record American*, a tabloid, read: DEB SEIZED FOR MURDER.

The story, as does the number-one story of most tabloids, appeared on page three:

Post-debutante Suzanne Clift, a 21-year-old Beacon Hill girl, was arrested on a murder warrant early today in connection with the shooting death of her handsome Italian physicist boy friend. The attractive, disturbed girl, niece of movie actor Montgomery Clift, had been sought since the nude body of Pierce B. Brentani [*sic*], 27, was found in her padlocked bedroom in her socially prominent grandmother's town house at 85 Pinckney St. . . .

Day after day, Boston's newspapers continued to publish potential evidence, given out by the police. The *Record-American*, in a page-one headline, said that Miss Clift admitted the killing. The *Herald* told its readers that she had stolen the murder weapon at a wedding party.

In New York, the story was just as big. A headline in the New York *Mirror*, typically inaccurate, said: FIANCÉ SLAIN, SOCIETY GIRL QUIZZED. (The slain man was not Miss Clift's fiancé.) The next day, over a picture of Miss Clift, the *Mirror* said: "Portrait of a Deb Who Slew." In the accompanying story Miss Clift was described as a "confessed slayer of beau."

Back in Boston the police continued to furnish the newspapers with prejudicial information. The *Record-American* wrote:

The blonde girl, niece of actor Montgomery Clift, has confessed to the murder, police say. . . .

It was pointed out to the *Record-American* that Suzanne and the Swiss-Italian engineer had been keeping steady company for months and that he had suddenly decided to take a trip abroad. The fatal shooting followed this revelation. . . .

Finally, the *Herald*, to leave no doubt what it thought the motive was, printed: "Obviously pregnant, the 21-year-old post-debutante stood mute to charges . . . that she shot Piero Brentani."

That is the way the story went in the newspapers in Boston, New York, and probably in much of the rest of the country. They printed statements from the police, from her attorney, and much evidence that ultimately would have been introduced into court. These stories ran for five months before she came to trial, five months during which the potential jurors of Boston were treated to revelations about the case having no bearing whatsoever on "the public's right to know."

Newspapers almost unanimously claim, in self-defense, that printing stories of this sort protects the public, makes it aware of perils, and helps it guard against future attacks. It is impossible to justify an explanation of this sort. The bare announcement of an unsolved murder is enough to put the public on its guard. The public, in fact, is so self-protective, that it will not come to the aid of people attacked in the streets in full view of witnesses. It does not need publication of potential evidence in a murder trial to know when to "look out." In any event, the kind of crime reporting discussed here refers to stories published *after* a suspect has been apprehended. If the suspect is already in custody when the stories appear, what further protection does the public need?

The stories about Suzanne Clift, though, went even beyond the kinds of unethical reporting described in other chapters.

What additional protection did the public have by learning that Suzanne Clift was "obviously pregnant," that Mr. Brentani's body was found nude, that she was the "niece of movie actor Montgomery Clift," and that she was the granddaughter of a socially prominent Boston woman? The public derived no protection from these stories. It was titilated by them—and they did no harm to the circulation figures of the newspapers that printed them.

There are dozens of other examples of celebrities getting treatment of this sort in the press. The "Fatty" Arbuckle case was one, a long time ago. More recently, Robert Mitchum was treated to national publicity on a relatively minor narcotics charge. Tony Martin was pilloried across the nation when he was indicted on charges of draft-dodging.

In 1958 came the low in reporting of this sort. The Los Angeles *Times* brought out an *extra* to announce, across the top of its front page:

DAUGHTER OF LANA TURNER KILLS MAN

Dapper Johnny Stompanato, 42, constant companion of Film Star Lana Turner, was stabbed to death last night by Lana's 14-year-old daughter Cheryl. . . .

Disclosure that the only child of the actress killed Miss Turner's constant companion of recent months was made by Police Chief Clinton Anderson . . .

Dept. Dist. Atty. Manley Browler said last night that Cheryl will be "treated no different than any other girl. She will be booked like any other juvenile and will be kept in Beverly Hills Jail overnight."

In later stories the paper was at pains to point out that the murder weapon was a ten-inch butcher's knife, that Cheryl Crane had deliberately gone to the kitchen to get it, and that she "plunged it into his abdomen."

The Los Angeles *Times* also took the trouble to find out that, a year earlier, Cheryl Crane had run away from a boarding school. When the police found her, they took her to the station until her parents came for her. The *Times* chose to headline those facts this way: CHERYL TURNED OVER TO POLICE ONCE BEFORE.

In the body of the story, the *Times* said:

. . . But, it wasn't the first time the girl, a student at the fashionable Happy Valley School in Ojai, had been in a police station.

Then it went on to tell the very much less sensational fact that she had run away from school, as many girls do.

These stories continued on page one of the Los Angeles *Times* every day, from the day of the arrest until the day a jury cleared Cheryl Crane by declaring the killing "justifiable homicide."

During those days the *Times* made it clear that Lana Turner had gone through four husbands, that she had spent two months in Acapulco, Mexico, with the murdered man (who was not her husband), that he had high connections in the underworld, and that the final fight—and killing—took place in Miss Turner's bedroom.

On almost any day of any week it is possible to pick up a newspaper and read of a killing by a teen-ager. Sometimes it is gang warfare, sometimes the motive is robbery, and sometimes it is a sex-killing. Most times the story is complete in two or three paragraphs, and usually the entire story is on an inside page.

Cheryl Crane, a child—but the child of a celebrity—was worth more attention. The more attention paid to Cheryl Crane, the more readers for the Los Angeles *Times*.

It takes the help of the press to create a celebrity. The press is always ready to collect for its help.

ELEVEN

The Defendant: His Legal Shields

D OES A DEFENDANT who has been "tried by newspaper" have any legal protection to help him when he gets to court?

Are there ways he can mitigate the effects of pre-trial publicity?

Does the law officially recognize that publicity can exercise a devastating effect on the possibility of a fair trial for a defendant?

The answer to all these questions is "yes"—with qualifications. Our laws are old. The protections written into them are not born of the mid-twentieth century, with its international-communications satellites, television, automatic typesetting machines, picture phones, and supersonic jet transports. Our laws, like so many other facets of our lives, have not kept pace with time.

Many of the legal shields available to a defendant might have been effective at one time. They are not now. Moreover, one is forced to wonder how really effective they ever were. Even in the eighteenth century a juror could read a newspaper article and form an opinion based on it.

Nonetheless, our lawmakers did foresee the possibility of a community so inflamed by publicity that impartial jurors, for all practical purposes, would be unavilable.

First, of course, came our Constitution. It guarantees: "In all criminal prosecutions, the accused shall enjoy the right to a speedy and public trial, by an impartial jury . . ." Out of this phrase came eight basic safeguards for the defendant.

A defendant can rely on 1) change of venue, 2) change of venire, 3) continuance, 4) severance, 5) *voir dire* examination, 6) challenges, 7) isolation of the jury, and 8) instructions to the jury. The safeguards exist. The issue is, how strong are they?

A request for a change of venue is a request that the trial be shifted from the locality where the crime was committed to another place, a place theoretically unaffected by the publicity.

Almost without exception, it is the defense that moves for a change of venue, when local passions seem so strong that a fair trial would be impossible. The motion is made to the presiding judge. If he agrees that it would be impossible to choose an impartial jury he will grant the change, transferring the trial to a city where, hopefully, the potential jurors have not formed opinions about the case.

In the days before radio, television, and the instantaneous delivery of newspapers with news from all over the world, a venue change could have meant a real difference in the attitude of a jury and its eventual verdict. That is not so any longer.

Except for crimes of a minor nature, crimes not sensational enough to attract more than local attention and local-newspaper stories, no community is so isolated that it does not hear about the case. Where, for example, could the Sam

THE DEFENDANT: HIS LEGAL SHIELDS

Sheppard trial have been moved? Where could the Lindbergh trial have been held, or the Rosenberg trial, the Hoffa trials, and so many others?

Additionally, most criminal cases are tried under state laws. This means that even if a change of venue is granted the trial is moved only to another city within the same state. If the publicity in the original city is so great that a change of venue is granted, that same publicity almost certainly covers the entire state. The change becomes meaningless. Thus, in all but minor cases, a change of venue is no longer adequate to guarantee a fair trial.

Frequently, though, the problem is not where to take the trial, but how to persuade a judge that a change of venue is necessary. How, after all, does a defense attorney prove to a judge that the jurors are not impartial, particularly when prospective jurors sincerely believe that they have not been influenced by what they have read or heard previously.

Only infrequently do judges grant these requests. They feel that their instructions to a jury will drive out all prejudice. That this is, at best, a tenuous hope is demonstrated by none other than an editorial writer. Mr. John Lofton, of the Pittsburg *Post-Gazette*, wrote:

The subject for main concern is the direct effect of criminal-trial reporting and comment by the press. In most cases jurors are not sequestered but are simply directed by the judge not to read, look at or listen to anything bearing on the case. A Washington, D.C., attorney has observed that "all jurors read newspapers and listen to radio and television, or at least talk to others who would have done so. No amount of warning by the trial judge will change that."

Most judges, also, hesitate to grant changes of venue because of the expense and inconvenience, certainly inhuman grounds in so critical a matter. Their hesitation makes a guilty verdict more likely.

Many defense attorneys appeal to an appellate court if they lose a case after having been denied a change of venue. Such an appeal says, in effect, that the judge committed an error in refusing to grant a venue change. There is no guarantee, though, that the appeals court will agree. The appeals court, too, must be shown that impartial jurors were unavailable, and why they were unavailable, before it will rule that the trial judge was in error. In outrageous cases, as *Irvin v. Dowd* (Chapter One), it is easily demonstrable. But in most cases it is not.

The appellate court cannot examine the original jurors. The defense can only present copies of newspaper stories and transcripts of radio and television broadcasts, and hope that the judges on the bench will see for themselves what the climate of opinion must have been at the time of the trial. Then, even if the appellate court does reverse the conviction, it means a new trial for the defendant—with all the attendant costs for the prosecution and the defense.

There is no reason for tranquility on the part of a defendant who, to overcome prejudicial pre-trial publicity, places his hopes in a change of venue. Yet, change of venue is regarded as the strongest of the legal safeguards available to a defendant.

Six of our fifty states authorize a change of venire. Simply, this is a switch on the change of venue. Instead of moving the trial to a different location, jurors are brought in from another town.

The hope, plainly, is that strange jurors from a strange town will be uninfected by the prejudices stirred up by pre-trial publicity in the town where the crime was committed.

But, to paraphrase a motion-picture title, no town is a stranger. Change of venire has proven to be as ineffective as a change of venue, and for the same reasons.

Beyond that, a change of venire is a much greater expense to the state. Jurors must be paid all their expenses, in addition to their daily fee. The expense, however, would be a piddling stumbling block if the system worked. It does not. Motions for change of venire are made very infrequently.

If a defense attorney loses his motion for a change of venue (or venire) or has no faith in its usefulness, he is apt to ask for a continuance. This substitutes a change in time for a change in geography.

The theory behind it is that the most inflamed passions die down with the passage of time. People tend to feel less vindictive. They forget the stories they have read, the gossip they have heard, the outrage they felt at the time the crime was committed. Prejudice departs and objectivity sets in.

This might be true in minor offenses. But minor offenses don't attract huge numbers of newspaper stories. Those cases that do make headlines day after day remain with the reader too long to enable the defendant to get the "speedy" trial to which he is entitled.

There are not many people who will soon forget the name Christine Keeler, or what she was tried for. Or names such as Hall, Mills, Thaw, Nesbitt, White, some of which have not been in the news for forty years or more.

Even if we did forget the names and the circumstances of their crime, would we not find ourselves reminded of them as the trial date drew closer? Would not an approaching trial constitute news, and therefore again become subject matter for newspaper and television reports? Would not the entire cycle begin again? At best, then, a continuance is a haphazard

hope for a defendant who has seen his name, his record, and
official comments about him in the press day after day.

A very minor form of protection—minor because it affects
so few people—is the motion for a severance. This applies in
cases involving two or more defendants. If one of the defendants has been the subject of a great deal of prejudicial publicity, the other(s) can ask for a severance—a separate trial—to
avoid the possibility of guilt by association.

A severance is not possible, of course, if the defendants
have been accused of a joint crime; conspiracy, for example,
which by definition must involve all the defendants at once.
The very existence, however, of "severance" is an implicit
admission that adverse publicity can affect the outcome of a
trial. This protection can be quite helpful to the defendant
who was not publicized. But what about the fellow who got
all the publicity? Obviously, the motion for severance does
not help the man who really needs the help.

Before any trial begins, the prospective jurors must submit
to a legal process called the *voir dire*. In the *voir dire* the judge
questions the veniremen in an attempt to learn whether or not
they have preconceived opinions about the case.

The judge also attempts to find out if the veniremen will be
able to disregard any preconceived notions they may have;
if they will be able to render a verdict based solely on the
evidence presented at the trial.

This entire process is based on faith alone. The prospective
juror must first admit that he has formed an opinion. If the
trial is one he particularly wants to sit on, it becomes very
tempting for him to deny having any opinions. What is more,
the denial can be—in the mind of the juror—truthful. He
may really believe that he has no opinions about the case, not
knowing what hidden influences are at work on his mind. Or

the denial can be untruthful—motivated by his strong desire to become a juror.

Even if he admits to a bias, he can promise the judge that he will disregard it. Judges tend to believe such promises, to seat the jurors who make them. Certainly this takes a lot for granted.

In *Lauderdale v. State*, while the judge was conducting the *voir dire*, a prospective juror admitted a preconceived notion about the case. The judge then asked, "You can and will set this preconceived opinion aside and go in the jury box with an open mind and try this case solely on the law and the evidence developed here and give both sides a fair and impartial trial?" The prospective juror replied, "That's correct."

The judge led that juror into his answer by the way he framed his question. The defendant in that case could be forgiven a few misgivings about the judge and the jury.

No one who takes a dispute to arbitration for settlement —be it a corporation-union fight, a disagreement between partners, or what have you—expects that the arbitrator will be someone who has an opinion concerning what the settlement should be, yet promises that his opinion will have no effect on his decision.

The two types of challenges available to counsel, challenges for cause and peremptory challenges, are still another protection written into our statutes.

Before a juror is seated both prosecution and defense counsel have a chance to question him, in much the same way the judge does on *voir dire*. The counsel can question veniremen about their backgrounds, their education, their work, or anything else in an attempt to find open or hidden bias. If either counsel finds demonstrable bias, or a basis for believing that it exists, he can prevent the seating of that person through a challenge for cause. As a matter of law, that person will not be seated. Moreover, each counsel is allowed a certain number of peremptory challenges. Without giving any reason at all, he can decide not to seat a particular person. These decisions are usually based on intuition, instinct, or hunches. But each counsel has only a limited number of peremptory challenges available. Once they are used up he must take the next jurors who come along unless he can prove to the judge that bias exists.

And, just as in the judge's *voir dire*, the counsel questioning a prospective juror must proceed on faith—on the hope that the answers are truthful.

Challenges are limited in the help they afford. In cases such as *Irvin v. Dowd* (Chapter One), or in any sensational case, they are not much help at all. Almost everyone available to serve on the jury has been prejudiced. The defense finds itself settling for those jurors who seem least affected.

Once a trial begins a judge can decide to isolate the jury, to keep it together day and night until the verdict is in. The jury trying Jack Ruby, in Dallas, Texas, was isolated.

Isolated juries cannot go home, cannot read uncensored newspapers or watch newscasts on television. Nor can they discuss among themselves the case they are sitting on. A court official remains with them at all times. They sleep (at least in Dallas) in tiny, windowless rooms about seven feet wide and ten feet long, just enough room for a bed, a sink, and a commode.

It may be comforting to know that your jury is locked up and cannot read newspaper accounts of the trial. This is no guarantee, however, that they have not read all the pre-trial stories about the case. Since it is pre-trial publicity that does the most damage, locking a jury up for the duration of a trial is a rather futile gesture. (It also makes many people try especially hard to get out of serving on a jury at all, a too common practice as it is.)

We come, then, to a judge's instructions to the jury. One such instruction, from Justice Bernard S. Meyer, was quoted in Chapter One. Generally, they are similar. Judges instruct the jury to render their verdict only on the basis of the evidence presented in the courtroom, and not to read or listen to stories concerning the case. How effective are the instructions, though, and how truthful are the jurors in responding to them?

A case in point is *Smith v. United States.*

Mr. Louis Smith was on trial for income-tax evasion. He had reported an income of $3,690.04. The government charged that his income was $39,984.49.

On the second day of the trial the St. Louis *Globe-Democrat* printed an inflammatory article and Smith's counsel moved for a mistrial. The court denied the motion, holding that the jurors had obeyed the court's instructions not to read newspaper accounts of the case. The defense counsel asked the judge to find out if the jurors had followed his instructions. The judge then ordered, "If any juror violated the instructions of the court and read the article . . . hold up your hand."

No juror held up his hand. Can one imagine that defendant Smith, sitting in court knowing that these articles had appeared, felt that his right to a fair trial had been ensured by the way that the question was posed?

In *United States v. Carlucci*, nine jurors *admitted* to disobeying the court's instructions.

Victor Carlucci and others were convicted of receiving and exporting firearms stolen from the federal government. They appealed for a reversal of their convictions because extensive, prejudicial stories appeared during the trial.

The court refused to reverse, holding that to grant a reversal would mean that virtually all juries from then on would have to be locked up and isolated during the course of a trial. That is like saying, "Well, it happened, but it is impossible to correct it so we'll let it go."

William Hastie, one of the judges sitting on that appeals court, dissented:

The case was tried to a jury for more than three weeks. During this period the jury was not sequestered. . . . During the first week of the trial derogatory articles about the defendants appeared, conspicuously placed and headlined, in local daily newspapers. The articles contained a substantial amount of material prejudicial to the defendants which was not and, in large part, could not have been put in evidence at the trial. As to this there is no dispute. The newspaper stories stated that all of the defendants were connected with a "gambling combine" . . . that one of them also operated a gambling concession in Havana, and that the purpose of their attempted exportation of guns was to protect gambling franchises in Cuba.

Nine jurors admitted that they had read these stories. And they all quickly agreed with one of their group who said he had "noticed the headlines, just noticed them and then just simply paid no further attention, other than those things you must scan quickly as you look at it. I didn't look to remember it."

Judge Hastie went on to say that the jurors obviously didn't wish to admit their wrongs, consequently tried to minimize their misdeeds with the above excuse. Carlucci's conviction stood.

Judge Simon H. Rifkind, commenting on instructions to jurors, says:

Some of my colleagues caution the jurors not to read the papers or listen to the radio during the trial. Not only does the warning usually come a little late, but if you are dealing with a celebrated cause in which juror John Doe sees his name in the newspapers for the first time in his life it is probably futile. To prevent that man from reading the papers will result in his death from frustration. You might just as well ask Katharine Hepburn not to read her press notices following an opening night.

These, then, are the legal shields available to a defendant in his search for a fair trial. That they are inadequate is demonstrated by the continuing pressures of respected groups within the legal profession for new and more stringent ways of ensuring "the right to a speedy and public trial, by an impartial jury."

TWELVE

Civilization or Barbarism,
Old World or New

OUR CONSTITUTION was revolutionary in its origins, revolutionary in its design, and, because of its success, revolutionary in its effect on the rest of the world. Nevertheless, it is only in the broadest sense that we are governed by the Constitution. The criminal laws we live under in our day-by-day existence are not the least bit revolutionary. They were borrowed well-nigh intact from the English common law. We were fortunate in our choice of that source; these laws serve us well.

However, despite the source to which we turned for our laws, we had fought a revolution to win freedoms the British did not allow; our zeal for liberty led us into certain departures from the British codes. We wanted more and better of particular freedoms. Among these was freedom of the press. Our press operates under fewer restrictions than does any other national press in the world. In view of our success as a democracy this is not totally bad; it is not idle chatter, or chauvinism, when the residents of our Fourth Estate say, "There is no freedom without freedom of the press."

There are jurists in this country who feel that in the area of crime reporting we should have stayed closer to the English system. They feel that press license could be somewhat modified without adversely affecting our liberties or our democracy. The English impose such restraints on their newspapers, and undeniably freedom of the press in England does not suffer because of them. Nor do any other English institutions commonly associated with democracy suffer because the English press is limited in the ways it can report crime news. (As a matter of fact, there are many subtle infringements on freedom in the United States, despite our free press, which don't exist in England at all. Fascists, Communists and what have you are professionally and socially acceptable in England. In certain professions in our country, however, it is sure starvation to admit to being a Communist.) It is, therefore, difficult to accept the argument of our press that we cannot modify its right to publish certain kinds of crime stories without running the concurrent risk of becoming a dictatorship. We have the experience of others as a standard. If it did not happen in England, why must it happen here?

The English press is absolutely forbidden to publish anything that might in any way interfere with a defendant's right to a fair trial. The newspapers themselves are subject to large fines if they commit contempt of court by printing prejudicial stories. Publishers, editors, and reporters are subject to fines, too, but they also risk jail sentences.

The English courts enforce these restrictions with great vigor. The result is a climate conducive to a fair trial. Nor is there any feeling that a defendant is "coddled," a bogey voiced very frequently and vociferously on this side of the Atlantic. The defendant in England is neither coddled nor victimized. He is, simply, a defendant in a criminal proceeding. It is up to the jury, and to no one else, to hear the facts and to determine innocence or guilt. The jury hears the facts, and only admissible facts, in court. Not in newspapers, on radio, or on television.

In January, 1965, the government of England disclosed plans to put further restrictions on press coverage of criminal cases. Under the new proposal, newspapers would not be permitted to publish testimony given against defendants in preliminary hearings. Even though these hearings are part of the judicial process, and take place under the supervision of the court, they are not part of the process of arriving at a verdict. Hence any information to come out of the hearings could, if learned by potential jurors, influence that verdict. In the future, in describing a preliminary hearing, British newspapers will be limited to reporting the name of the accused, the charge against him, and the court's decision to dismiss or to hold the defendant for trial. *That* is regard for justice.

There are contempt procedures in the United States, too. Unfortunately, these procedures are considerably weakened both by lack of enforcement and by a constant series of Supreme Court reversals of earlier citations. The Supreme Court, as we will see, places great stress on freedom of speech when it is asked to rule on the role played by particular newspapers in particular cases.

The differences between the English system and our own are clearly illustrated by a contempt citation, in England, involving the international edition of *Newsweek* magazine.

It involved the famous case of Dr. John Bodkin Adams, the doctor who was accused of murdering one of his patients in order to get her out of the way before she could change her will—in which she left a large sum of money to him! Scotland Yard suspected him of murdering several other patients for the same reason. He was prosecuted for only one murder, that of Mrs. Edith Morrell, because the prosecution felt that it had an extremely good, almost unassailable case against him.

The international edition of *Newsweek*, the edition sold in England, carried virtually intact the story printed in the American edition, which said:

BRITAIN:
THE DOCTOR ON TRIAL

In his 34 years of general practice in Eastbourne, a quiet English seaside resort, Dr. John Bodkin Adams had, by British medical standards, done surprisingly well. When he arrived penniless from Belfast in northern Ireland in 1922, a group of local doctors had taken up a collection to buy medical instruments for him. Now he lived in a big house on fashionable Trinity Trees. He employed three servants, and a chauffeur to drive his MG or Rolls-Royce on visits to his elderly patients, a remarkable number of whom remembered him in wills when they died. Over a period of twenty years, seventeen of Dr. Adams' grateful patients bequeathed to him the sum total of $90,000 and this was what started the teacups rattling in Eastbourne. Gossipers whispered. Could it be possible that Dr. Adams had helped some of these elderly sufferers along to a quiet, respectable death?

A sort of fascinated panic gripped Eastbourne last year when Scotland Yard's immaculate, storybook sleuth, Herbert (the Count) Hannan, turned up to investigate the rumors. Hannan spent several weeks in town studying 300-odd wills. Then one day he marched into Adams' consulting room and placed him under arrest for the murder of Mrs. Edith Morrell, an 81-year-old widow who died on November 13, 1950 . . .

Dr. Adams was charged with murder through the use of "massive quantities" of drugs. . . .

Last week, the trial of John Bodkin Adams began in London's famous Old Bailey. . . .

Climbing the stairs from Cell No. 23, the defendant

emerged blinking in the sudden light of the world's oldest court of criminal justice. Ignoring the clerk who asked him to state his formal plea, Adams looked straight at the red-robed, white-wigged presiding judge and said firmly, "I am not guilty, my Lord."

The prosecution's lofty tower of evidence quickly collapsed under the courteous but devastating cross-examination of defense counsel Geoffrey Lawrence. . . .

The pink-cheeked physician was so elated over the first week's testimony that he threw a champagne party in his cell for his brilliant defense team.

Newsweek then printed a second article:

BEQUESTS

Eastbourne's frenzied gossip pushed Dr. Adams' alleged victims as high as 400. Attention focused on: Edith Alice Morrell, 81. Died in 1950, leaving Adams her Georgian silver. Her son gave him her Rolls-Royce.

—Alfred John Hullett, 71. Died in March, 1956, left Adams $1,400.

—Gertrude Joyce Hullett, 50, his widow. Died four months after her husband, left Adams $2,800 and a bigger, newer Rolls-Royce. When Adams tried to arrange a private post-mortem for her, the coroner asked, "When did she die?" Adams replied: "She hasn't died yet."

The international edition of *Newsweek*, with these facts in it, appeared in England while Dr. Adams' trial was in progress. The court termed it "highly prejudicial matter." (It seems tame, actually, when compared to some of the news stories, cited elsewhere in this book, published by American newspapers.)

The court wanted to bring *Newsweek* to account, to cite it for contempt. But *Newsweek* was registered in Dayton, Ohio, and had no responsible manager or editor in England. Consequently, the English court could find no jurisdiction over the magazine itself.

However, the court did bring in Eldon Wylie Griffiths, senior representative and chief European reporter for *Newsweek*. Mr. Griffiths' job was to send news stories to the magazine's headquarters in New York.

Also ordered into court were Rolls House Publishing Company, Ltd., the English importers of the magazine, and W. H. Smith & Son, Ltd., news agents who had sold about 1,800 copies of the magazine at their newsstands.

Neither Rolls nor Smith had known that that issue of *Newsweek* contained the contemptuous article about the trial. As soon as authorities called their attention to it, they withdrew the magazine from circulation. In court they argued that they should not be held in contempt since they had not known that the magazines contained prejudicial information.

The court disagreed. It concluded that Rolls House Publishing and W. H. Smith & Son should be held in contempt because it was their duty to know what they were selling. The court felt, too, that magazines not subject to the jurisdiction of English courts might feel no obligation to respect British laws in the matter of crime reporting if Rolls and Smith were not penalized. Both were fined.

Griffiths contended in court that the *Newsweek* story was an attempt by its editors to tell the events of the trial accurately and impartially. The court responded: "We can only say their performance seems lamentably inconsistent with their intentions. . . . It is safe to say there is not a newspaperman in Great Britain who would not have seen at a glance that these paragraphs were objectionable in the highest degree and would expose those responsible for them to the risk of severe punishment." Griffiths, however, was not held in contempt because the court felt that he was in no way responsible for the articles.

Dr. John Bodkin Adams was acquitted by the jury.

An American must wonder if Dr. Adams would have been acquitted by an American jury. A case of that sort, embodying all the elements of a classic mystery, would have been certain to receive equally classic coverage in our newspapers, both before and during the trial. We cannot be certain that our jurors would have remained unaffected by such stories. American jurors in other cases have freely admitted to bias on the basis of stories they had read before they went to court. The jurors who sat in judgment on Dr. Adams were not influenced by facts learned outside the courtroom. The facts they learned they heard in the courtroom. The court seemed lenient in the *Newsweek* case. It is usually much more severe.

Regina v. Odhams Press Ltd. shows just how severe English law can be in assessing punishment to purveyors of pre-trial publicity. *The People,* a newspaper published by Odhams Press, had been running a series of stories on brothel keepers. In one particular issue it concentrated on a man named Anthony Micallef, taking him to task for the way he earned his livelihood. The article attacked Micallef for being in the business of purveying vice and managing street women. It said that Micallef had boasted that he was private secretary and accountant to a gang of brothel keepers. The article concluded by urging that Micallef be arrested and prosecuted.

Micallef, though, had already been arrested on vice charges. Micallef had been arrested in June, 1956, and charged with brothel keeping. It was on July 15 that *The People* (Odhams Press), whose circulation was 4,000,000 per week, published its article headlined: ARREST THIS BEAST.

Henry Ainsworth, editor, and Duncan Webb, a reporter,

who were called to account by the court for publishing the story, had not known when they printed it that Micallef had been arrested. In their own defense they said that since they had not known of Micallef's arrest they obviously could not have realized that their story would be prejudicial to a fair trial for Micallef. In court Ainsworth and Webb admitted that the material was prejudicial. They apologized to the court for publishing it, but felt that they should not be held in contempt of court since they had not intended to interfere with the defendant's rights.

The court disagreed. It said that Ainsworth and Webb had a duty to find out whether or not a person who was the subject of an article calling attention to that person's lawlessness had been arrested. It said further that the defendant's intent was irrelevant. What was relevant was that prejudicial material had been published and the defendant's right to a fair trial impaired. The court fined Ainsworth and Webb £500 (about $1,500) each.

One might compare the severity of this punishment with the complete lack of punishment in similar cases in our country—in the Sheppard case, or in *People v. Stroble*, where newspapers called Stroble a "werewolf" and published his confession before his trial, or the case of George Whitmore, Jr., or any of the others cited in chapters to come.

English law is so strong in this regard that it cares not only about actual harm done to a defendant, but also about the *possibility* of harm resulting from prejudicial publicity. The *possibility* of harm was the reason for *Regina v. Evening Standard Co. Ltd.*

In February of 1954 a man named Kemp was indicted for murdering his wife. As part of its case against Kemp, the Crown produced one witness, a Miss Briggs, who testified that

Kemp had told her he had never been married. Another
Crown witness, a Mrs. Darmody, testified that Kemp had told
her he had been married, but that his wife had died. Neither
Miss Briggs nor Mrs. Darmody testified to anything else.

That evening, the *Evening Standard* printed:

TRUNK TRIAL: STORY OF MARRIAGE OFFER—HUSBAND IS ACCUSED

Mrs. Gertrude Darmody, of Spitalfields, Norwich, said at
the assizes [trial] here that a man accused of murdering his
wife asked her to marry him. "He told me he was not married.
After I had seen him in the same public house again and he
had asked me to marry him, I asked him to show me his army
pay-book."

The story was carried over to the back page, where the
carry-over headline said: ACCUSED MAN "ASKED ME TO MARRY."

The story was totally inaccurate. Mrs. Darmody had not
testified that Kemp had proposed to her. The reporter confused her testimony with an incident regarding the other witness, Miss Briggs. Miss Briggs, *out of the presence of the jury*,
had offered to prove in court that Kemp had asked her to
marry him. The judge refused to admit her evidence on the
grounds that it would prejudice the jury, and had nothing to
do with whether or not Kemp had murdered his wife. Thus,
the newspaper story not only put nonexistent words in Mrs.
Darmody's mouth, it also printed the prejudicial material that
the judge had ruled inadmissible. (Preceding pages have
shown many examples of American newspapers doing exactly
that.)

The morning after the article appeared, Kemp's defense
lawyer brought the article to the judge's attention. The lawyer
did not, however, press for a new trial because he felt that it
would be impossible to empanel a new jury uninfluenced by

the story. He hoped, too, that so much had already been established in Kemp's defense that the existing jury would place little faith in the story. The jury acquitted Kemp. It found him "not guilty."

Despite Kemp's acquittal, the *government* (not the court) asked that the publisher of the *Evening Standard* be held in contempt. The court agreed, saying:

> The fact that the prisoner was acquitted of the murder is neither here nor there; fortunately no damage was done to him, although that is not a matter which concerns the court, because the question is one of much more far-reaching importance than that.

The publisher of the *Evening Standard*, in his defense, said that his reporter, an experienced and trusted member of the newspaper's staff for ten years, had simply become confused by all the events at the trial, and had mixed up Mrs. Darmody's testimony in court with Miss Briggs's statements out of court. He maintained that the court should not take jurisdiction over the case.

In this instance, the court disagreed, saying:

> This is surely a proper matter to bring before this court. It is just as well that the nature of the jurisdiction which this court exercises on these occasions with regard to reports of trials in newspapers should be understood. It is called contempt of court, and that is a convenient expression because it is akin to a contempt. But the essence of the jurisdiction is that reports, if they contain comments on cases before they are tried, or alleged histories of the prisoner who is on trial . . . are matters which *tend to interfere with the due course of justice*. The foundation of the jurisdiction is that such reports are an interference with the due course of justice. [italics added]

The government of England thus established as its criterion that a story need only "tend to interfere with the due course of justice." When will the U.S. Government, or any one of the fifty states, take it upon itself to fight for the rights of a defendant—rather than wait for the defendant to appeal on his own?

Even though the defendant was acquitted the story *could have been* so prejudicial that it met the aforementioned criterion set by the court. The publisher of the *Evening Standard* was fined £1,000 (almost $3,000).

In terms of inaccurate reporting, a situation very similar to the case described above occurred in New York. In *United States v. Leviton* the defendants were indicted for exporting *wheat flour and lard* to Italy. They were convicted.

After the conviction, four copies of the New York *Times* were found in the jury room. The *Times* reported that the defendants had been indicted for exporting $9,500 worth of *barbed wire,* and that they'd tried to bribe a customs officer with an offer of $200.

There had never been a mention of a bribe, either in the indictment or in the trial. And the indictment had nothing to do with barbed wire.

Yet the *Times* suffered no penalty. There seems little doubt that were our press governed by laws similar to those in England, the *Times* would have been subject to an action for contempt. For good reason.

English concern over this problem antedates the very existence of the United States. As early as 1742, in *Roach v. Garvin,* the court said:

Nothing is more incumbent upon courts of justice than to preserve their proceedings from being misrepresented; nor is there anything of more pernicious consequence, than to prej-

udice the minds of the public against persons concerned as
parties in cases, before the cause is finally heard. . . .

There are three different sorts of contempt. One kind of
contempt is, scandalizing the court itself. There may be likewise a contempt of this court in abusing parties who are concerned in causes here. There may be also a contempt of this
court, in prejudicing mankind against persons, before the
cause is heard.

Halsbury's Laws of England says:

The issuing of attachment by the supreme courts of justice
for contempts out of court is founded upon the same im-
memorial usage as supports the whole fabric of common
law. . . .

It has also been held that, for a criminal prosecution to be
pending for this purpose, it is not necessary for the accused to
have been committed for trial, or even for him to have been
before a court of summary jurisdiction; provided that he has
been arrested and is in custody; and the opinion has been
expressed that it is not necessary for a cause actually to be
begun since, if it be imminent, it is possible "very effectively to
poison the fountain of justice before it begins to flow."

Apropos of that, the *Evening Standard* seems to have
missed an earlier chance to learn its lesson. In 1924 it had
been involved in a similar case.

It had joined with several other newspapers to hire an
amateur detective to investigate a crime. When the amateur
detective turned in his reports, the papers printed them. The
actual defendant was, at that point, under arrest and awaiting
trial.

That contempt cost the *Standard* £1,000 (in those days
equivalent to $5,000).

India, Pakistan, Australia, even Iraq, that bastion of civilized behavior, prescribe what the press cannot do to a defendant.

In Nazi Germany the government *encouraged* the press to print defamatory comments about certain defendants before trial.

Perhaps in England, a guilty defendant has some reason to feel he might "beat the rap," because of the protections afforded him against prejudicial publicity. But compare him to the innocent defendant in this country, who sees his name in headlines dozens of times before trial.

Which is the more civilized system? Suppose you were the innocent defendant?

THIRTEEN

Status Quo or Remedy?

OUR GOVERNMENT guarantees the protection of any of its nationals caught overseas by an unfriendly government. Theoretically, we stand ready to go to any lengths short of war to protect one of our own.

When Robert Vogeler, an American citizen, was arrested by the Hungarian Government for alleged spying, the United States entered into years-long negotiations in an attempt to free him. Eventually, he was freed.

William Oatis, another American citizen, was arrested by the Czechoslovakian Government while he was stationed in Prague as correspondent for the Associated Press. The State Department entered an immediate protest.

It was, at the outset, unavailing. There was no letup in effort, however, and ultimately we won freedom for Oatis by making a deal with the Czech Government. We agreed to repatriate a convicted Czech spy in return for Oatis' release from prison.

In both cases, and in others, our government stood behind the rights of its citizens—protected them from the incursions of foreign governments.

This same government guarantees every American citizen at home the right to a fair trial and to due process of law. This guarantee applies to every individual no matter what the crime, no matter how many confessions, no matter how guilty the police think he is.

Despite this constitutional guarantee, almost all journalists admit that somewhere there is a newspaper, a radio station, or a television station guilty of publishing, before a trial is held, information prejudicial to defendants. They will even admit that this should not exist. The difficulty is in finding journalists who want to do something positive about it.

The Fourth Estate stands foursquare for codes of ethics. It says in effect, "We can police ourselves." Anything beyond this is said to be the beginning of the end of freedom of the press, and when freedom of the press goes, of course, our other freedoms go with it.

By the same token, then, the chief opponents of legislative correction are the same members of the press who believe in codes of ethics. Mr. Felix McKnight (see Chapter Two) is representative of them. They ask for codes, but will not accept one with enforceable penalties against those who break them.

The Supreme Court Justice Arthur Goldberg, in a speech to the American Society of Newspaper Editors in 1964, said: "It would be most helpful in this area if this organization were to *revive* and *refurbish* [italics added] its existing code of ethics by adding specific standards of crime reporting which, while preserving complete freedom for the press, will also adequately safeguard the rights of an accused."

Justice Goldberg went on to cite the use of words such as "killer," "robber," and "hoodlum" in headlines and stories appearing right up until the eve of a trial. But he does not recommend specific solutions, or precise additions to the code of ethics. Nor does he say what he must, as a lawyer, believe —that codes without enforcement provisions are useless. Even the codes of the American Bar Association are backed by the possibility of disbarment.

One such code, the Massachusetts Bar-Press Guide, came into use in 1963. It lists seven restraints for the press to follow; but it begins weakly:

Newspapers in publishing accounts of crime should keep in mind that the accused may be tried in a court of law.

To preserve the individual's rights to a fair trial, news stories of crime should contain only a factual statement of the arrest and attending circumstances.

The following *should be avoided* [italics added]:

1. Publication of interviews with subpoenaed witnesses after an indictment is returned.

2. Publication of the criminal record or discreditable acts of the accused after an indictment is returned or during the trial unless made part of the evidence in the court record. The defendant is being tried on the charge for which he is accused and not on his record. (Publication of a criminal record could be grounds for a libel suit.)

3. Publication of confessions after an indictment is returned unless made a part of the evidence in the court record.

4. Publication of testimony stricken by the court, unless reported as having been stricken.

5. Editorial comment preceding or during trial, tending to influence judge or jury.

6. Publication of names of juveniles involved in juvenile proceedings unless the names are released by the judge.

7. The publication of any "leaks," statements or conclusions as to the innocence or guilt, implied or expressed, by the police or prosecuting authorities or defense counsel.

The code is exactly the same for broadcasters, except for the substitution of the word "broadcasting" for "publication."

This code provokes several questions. Why does it use the word "avoided"? Why not, instead, "The following should be prohibited"? Why, if the code is realistic, is the press not willing to make it law? Is it that a code is easily breakable, but that law is not? Why, if newspapers recognize those seven points as abuses which currently exist, are they unwilling to accept a law that would make it impossible, or at least illegal, to commit those abuses? If this code does not abridge freedom of the press (and obviously it does not or the Massachusetts press would not have signed it), then how would the same code, as law, be an abridgment?

Moreover, there are loopholes in the code. It is very careful to say that certain things—criminal records, confessions— should not be published "after an indictment is returned." But in most cases "after an indictment has been returned" is too late. Prejudicial information published before an indictment can affect a grand jury; indeed, might stimulate an indictment. Furthermore, prejudicial publicity followed by an indictment only serves to cement opinions already formed by the public.

Publication of testimony stricken by the court (point 4 in the code), even if so reported, is equally dangerous. The substance of the stricken testimony published in a newspaper story (and jurors, despite admonishment, read newspapers) might be so inflammatory that it would remain with the reader despite a judge's ruling that it was inadmissible. Furthermore, the code fails to tell us what would happen to a newspaper that broke the code.

But most important of all, only 26 of Massachusetts' 40 daily newspapers have agreed to adhere to the code. This leaves 14 newspapers free to publish anything they want to print. If these 14 newspapers start to cut into the circulation of the others, it is easy to guess what will happen to the code.

New Jersey, too, attempted to deal with prejudicial newspaper stories, through the New Jersey Supreme Court dictum banning all potentially prejudicial statements by prosecution, defense, and the police (see Chapter Three). This ban cannot be completely effective as long as its enforcement depends on the tracking down of the source of a statement. Newspaper reporters usually do not have to reveal the sources of their information, hence New Jersey newspapers, and others in nearby states, can still print leaks from irresponsible or self-interested officials. The culpable official is fairly safe and he knows it. The ban should obligate the newspapers, too, to be of really significant help.

That such a ban will be a long time in coming, if newspaper cooperation is a prerequisite, is suggested by Mr. Sam Ragan, president of the Associated Press Managing Editors Association, who said, "We are hearing again the ancient cry that the free press is the enemy of fair trial. The free press," he went on, "is the last defense before the Star Chamber and ultimately secret arrest and trial." As Mr. Ragan well knows, a star-chamber proceeding is possible only if the press is barred from courtrooms during trials. No one proposes that.

Ragan, executive editor of the Raleigh, North Carolina, *News and Observer-Times*, is not atypical of press-management thinking across the country.

Clifton Daniel, managing editor of the New York *Times*, said after New Jersey's Supreme Court issued its dictum, "We must do nothing to lessen competition, initiative and aggressiveness in pursuit of the news."

The New York *Post*, on November 18, 1964, lauded New Jersey's court in an editorial:

If it [New Jersey's order] is upheld in the higher courts, we will have moved appreciably closer to the British system. Pretrial press coverage of crimes will be less colorful, but the rights of the defendant to his day in court will be better protected. . . .

But on December 24, 1964, just over a month after it printed that editorial, the *Post* published this story.

FIND HEIRESS SLAIN:
COPS SEIZE SUSPECT

A 22-year-old unemployed mechanic was arrested early today in the rape-slaying of heiress Felice Bradley, 37, in her West Side apartment.

Police said [italics added here and below] the suspect, Robert Sims, is also being questioned about a series of rape-assaults in the Crown Heights section of Brooklyn. Sims bears a strong resemblance, *police said*, to the composite sketch provided by *Crown Heights witnesses.* . . .

The suspect allegedly admitted he was a heroin addict. *Police said* he had a "$30-a-day habit."

Police gave this account of Miss Bradley's murder: . . .

The story continues by giving a complete, incident-by-incident re-creation of the police version of the murder, naming Sims all the way through.

Yet, just the day before, on December 23, 1964, the *Post* had run a story on another man who had been arrested for the same Crown Heights rapes. In it, the *Post* quoted Police Inspector Albert Seedman: " 'This is definitely the Crown Heights rapist we have been looking for.' "

Neither man had been indicted. Both stories quoted police sources.

Editorials are pious and righteous. A newspaper's true character is limned in its news columns.

A rather eye-opening sidelight to this whole problem of pre-trial publicity occurred, also in New Jersey, also in December of 1964, in connection with a proposed conflict-of-interest law to govern New Jersey's state legislators. The bill proposed that a commission consisting of both state cabinet officers and state legislators conduct hearings whenever a legislator is accused of a breach of ethics. *But the initial hearing before the commission will be behind closed doors, to prevent publicity for what might be irresponsible charges.*

Apparently legislators are willing to protect their own against accusations in a press they admit is irresponsible, but not willing to protect anyone else against similar accusations in the same press. Self-preservation *is* the first law of that jungle.

The Philadelphia Bar Association officially recognized the problem of trial by newspaper in December, 1964, when one of its committees proposed a series of guide lines for the release to news media of information about criminal cases.

The Philadelphia code asks that news releases concerning criminal matters be made by the head of the police department or designated and authorized officials. It continues: "It is undesirable to furnish intimate and sordid details. The right of the public servants must be modified by the right of the victims to privacy and the right of defendants to a fair trial; and even by considerations of good taste."

It goes on to urge that, during the investigation of a crime, information should not be furnished unless it will help the investigation. For example:

The release of any information, however accurate, which would not be admissible at a future trial of the individual, should always be avoided.

It is recognized that in certain cases of great news interest there will be conflict between the needs of the news media and the obligations of the law enforcement authorities. Under such condition, it is felt that the police and/or prosecutors should refuse and the *press should not request:*

The right to review police records; the right to invade the Police department or the prosecutor's office; the right to demand photographs; the right to receive intimate and sordid details about the victims or the perpetrators of sensational crimes; the right to accompany police in the course of an investigation array, or round-up of suspects.

Further, the proposed code advises investigators to shun the giving of opinions prior to the arrest of a defendant and to avoid mentioning admissions of guilt or confessions. During a trial the police, the prosecution, and the defense should not make statements to the press, but should let the evidence speak for itself.

This code is not intended to be legally binding. It would merely set up guide lines to be carried out voluntarily. There is nothing in it which seems in any way unreasonable, or in any way destructive of democratic processes.

Within twenty-four hours of the release of the proposed code the Philadelphia Press Association, the Philadelphia Chapter of Sigma Delta Chi (the national journalistic fraternity), the district attorney of Philadelphia, the mayor of Philadelphia, and the police commissioner all came out in opposition.

The district attorney said that the bar association did not have the power to regulate the news media or his office. He added that the press usually has its own way of obtaining information that does not come from official sources. "Under no circumstances," he said, "can or should the press be prohibited from printing this, as long as it holds to the basic principles of responsibility and accuracy."

The mayor said: "The public's right to know is one of the

fundamentals of the American way of life. A free flow of information to the public is a responsibility and a necessity. A blanket of secrecy is a grave danger to any people, as we see tragically in other parts of the world."

The police commissioner argued that the only guide lines should be those of good taste.

The proposals of the criminal law committee of the Philadelphia Bar Association, weak as they stand, would be quite strong if they were law rather than code. Yet, as weak as they are, they are opposed by groups and individuals who proclaim allegiance to the American way of life. Somehow these people, in their haste to make rhetoric, forget that the American way of life is defined by the degree of dignity accorded each person. And that covers suspects as well as Medal of Honor winners; some suspects have been Medal of Honor winners.

Connecticut, too, through an order issued by Jon O. Newman, United States Attorney for the Connecticut District, may soon see some progress in this field. In December, 1964, Mr. Newman ordered all federal prosecutors in Connecticut not to make public statements that might be considered prejudicial to defendants before or during trials. *This ban covers the disclosure of a defendant's criminal record, confessions, statements of witnesses, reports of investigative agencies, and opinions of the prosecutors themselves.* It prohibits the disclosure of the "existence or nature" of evidence bearing on the guilt of a suspect or a defendant.

Mr. Newman's order allows Connecticut's federal prosecutors to disclose the "fact and essential circumstances of an arrest, the name, address and age of all adult defendants, the nature of the charge, and all events occurring in the judicial process which are matters of public record." It goes on:

Close questions as to what may appropriately be disclosed are to be resolved against disclosure and in favor of protecting the accused's right to a fair trial. To put it simply, if in doubt, keep silent. . . .

Defendant has a right to have the issue of his innocence or guilt determined by a jury that is free of the prejudice so easily stirred by publicity before and during a trial.

The public has a right to know that the laws are being enforced, that suspects are being apprehended, that trials are being conducted and that the guilty are being convicted and punished.

This, like the New Jersey Supreme Court dictum, is an excellent beginning. It is, however, in many ways less than the best. Firstly, it does not effect any of the local or state prosecutors in Connecticut; only those working for the federal government. It is not specific, but leaves to the discretion of the individual what may or may not be disclosed. "If in doubt, keep silent," is hardly an ironclad proscription. Neither does it spell out the penalties to be applied to the federal prosecutor caught "leaking" information. Indeed, it does not deal at all with the problem of reporters who are "privileged" not to disclose the sources of their information, thus protecting the prosecutor who wants to leak information.

It is difficult to understand, too, why this order was not sent out from Washington, to cover federal prosecutors in all fifty states. Certainly if the order is a good one it should not apply only to Connecticut.

Nevertheless, that some states are witnessing the beginnings of an attempt to solve the problem of pre-trial publicity is heartening.

Yet despite this apparent progress there are some, even in the legal profession, who maintain that the problem does not exist. One such is Claude R. Sowle, Associate Dean and Professor of Law at Northwestern University Law School. In a speech to the City Club of Chicago, in June 1964, he said:

In any year in Chicago, one can probably count on the fingers of his two hands the cases in which the harms—either real or imagined—of pre-trial press coverage can seriously be raised. Unless the nature and circumstances of a crime are highly unusual or the persons involved enjoy a very special status in the community, it is unlikely that the press will devote much, if any, attention to a particular case. . . .

I happen to believe that when a juror takes the oath and states that he is capable of rendering a fair verdict, he will generally do everything within his power to follow the judge's instructions as to the law and return a verdict which is based on the evidence presented in court. Do the fair trial-oriented press restrictionists doubt this? If so, they would do well to forget about the press and turn their attention to the basic question of trial by jury, the foundations upon which our system of criminal justice rests. . . .

Dean Sowle counts on the fingers of his two hands the number of people, in Chicago, harmed by pre-trial press coverage in any given year. Going back only to the beginning of this century, that would mean 640 people in Chicago alone. Multiply that by the twenty largest cities in our country and we would have 12,800 people conceivably harmed by unfair press treatment. And this would cover only our largest cities, and only since the turn of the century. Even if it were only the ten people the good dean equates with the fingers of his hands that would be ten too many.

His belief that jurors can render a fair verdict based only on the testimony they've heard in court flies in the face of facts established and admitted by jurors themselves. He is on stronger ground when he suggests a re-examination of the jury system.

And what would Dean Sowle say about the chance Lee Harvey Oswald would have had for a fair trial? Or Sam Sheppard's actual trial? Or the trial of Leslie Irvin?

While Dean Sowle speaks for an apparent minority of lawyers, John Harrison, associate editor of the Toledo *Blade*, speaks for a minority of newspapermen. In an article in the *Saturday Review* he wrote:

Yet the freedom newspapers enjoy never has been an unlimited privilege. In two hundred and some years of flowering, it has been nurtured in the public's name. It is for the citizenry that the press speaks when it demands to know how the public's business is transacted, how justice is administered. Where this freedom clearly transgresses other constitutional rights it can claim no priority. . . .

There are not many editors who do not recognize the nature of the conflict; but few can decide where full and objective reporting leaves off and the abuses that hinder a fair trial begin. And surely such professional newspaper groups as the American Society of Newspaper Editors, Sigma Delta Chi, and others ought to take the lead in promoting the kind of code that will reconcile these conflicts. . . .

To assure the public full information about public affairs, to prevent the suppression of individual rights which secrecy and censorship make possible, the press is free. It should remain so. If, however, even a few newspapers abuse this freedom the courts and, if need be, the legislatures, will impose restrictions. For it was never intended that freedom of the press should give newspapers license to cripple the right of every man to a fair trial.

Mr. Harrison, newspaperman, wrote this article in 1955. Ten years later, the progress he asks for has barely begun in the form of voluntary codes. One wonders when his prediction of legislative remedies will come to pass.

That they had not yet come to pass as 1964 ended caused

Richard Starnes, a nationally syndicated columnist, to take up the cudgels. Discussing the role of the press in the Lee Oswald case, he wrote:

Saddest of all is the fact that the Oswald case was unique only in its celebrity. The same thing happens every day, to the extent that one could almost adopt as a rule of thumb that no defendant in any notorious criminal case ever gets a wholly fair trial. Politically ambitious prosecutors, which include almost all the breed, systematically leak choice morsels to news media, and by the time the veniremen are seated the atmosphere is hopelessly clouded by unfair pre-trial publicity.

Newspaper people do not like to talk about this. They know it is true, and they know it makes it difficult for the criminal defendant to obtain a fair trial. But the thought of some quasi-judicial bureaucracy telling them what they may and may not print runs counter to their every instinct and they fight it. . . .

Starnes's point is, of course, that newspapers will never take steps of their own to correct their misdeeds. As if to prove his point, the New York *World-Telegram*, which printed Starnes's column, *on the very same day* printed the following editorial:

GAG ON CRIME NEWS

In Philadelphia, where the Constitution was written, the lawyers association has just adopted an amazing set of restrictions on crime news.

While these restrictions are euphemistically called "merely guide lines," they are enforceable by bar association censure of lawyers or judges who transgress them. . . .

It was all done, ostensibly, in the name of protecting the accused, of avoiding so-called "trial by newspapers."

But, as the Pennsylvania Chief Justice said, it is law-abiding persons and not the perpetrators of crime who are entitled to increased protection by the police, public officials and the courts . . . All those accused are presumed innocent until convicted. Honest trials are the essence of justice. Both these ingredients of fair play are far more likely if all the informa- courts. . . . All those accused are presumed innocent until tion is known and understood by the public. . . .

There is nothing incompatible between the public's right to know about crime and the rights of those charged with crime. . . .

On the basis of the above editorial, the *World-Telegram* apparently is not about to make things more equitable for a defendant.

Also addressing himself to the problem of trial by news- paper, Turner Catledge, executive editor of The New York *Times,* has declared:

We live in an open society and one of the greatest things that keeps a society is the free use and free reading of its newspapers. In order to have free reading of newspapers, you have to have free publication of newspapers.

Some judgment has to be used, of course, on the part of the newspaper, but we cannot try criminal trials.

There is the competitive matter between newspapers, among newspapers themselves, between newspapers and other media, which is a matter of fact and which whets our efforts to get at news. . . .

I frankly don't know whether we can control that volun- tarily or not, but I'm awfully skittish of any general laws on the subject. . . . [italics added]

It is clear that if men like Turner Catledge will not propose solutions to the problem of trial by newspaper, we cannot look to newspapermen to put an end to the problem.

We have, by now, heard from practicing lawyers, district attorneys, bar associations, federal prosecutors, judges, and newspapermen. Of them all, those who present the only unified opposition to effective methods of dealing with trial by newspaper are the newspapermen themselves.

What, then, is the solution? Codes of ethics must be discarded because they lack strength. Another suggestion advanced by some jurists is the libel suit. Advocates of the libel suit point out that a defendant who feels he was the victim of prejudicial publicity prior to his trial can bring suit against the offending newspaper(s).

This proposal has several difficulties. What of the defendant who was really guilty, but who was also the victim of trial by newspaper? How does he sue for libel? Does he win a libel award and thereby, in a sense, profit from his crime? If the defendant is innocent, how does he, or a court, assess monetary damages?

The biggest objection, however, is the cost of the libel suit itself. Very few people can afford the legal fees involved in any kind of court proceeding. Libel cases are even worse. They tend to drag on for years, through several appeals, before a final decision. Attorneys charge large fees for work of this sort.

The cost of such a suit is frequently a deterrent to proceeding with it. It is too bad, but justice is sometimes unavailable to those who cannot afford it.

In late 1964, for example, Sugar Ray Robinson filed a libel suit for $1,000,000 against Walter Winchell and Hearst Consolidated Publications. Hearst's national editor, Frank Conniff, said, "If Robinson's going to tangle with our lawyers, then he's got more money than we think he has."

Recourse to libel suits is, therefore, a poor answer. It does nothing to eliminate the problem. The most even a successful libel suit can do is to mitigate a wrong already committed. The wrong must be eliminated, not mitigated.

For many years Justice Bernard S. Meyer (see Chapter One) of the New York State Supreme Court has sought a way to eliminate trial by newspaper. He has instigated professional study groups, joined committees and, as a member of the bench, studied the problem at first hand. He has lived with the effects of "the press's excesses."

His study has been thorough, exhaustive, and fruitful. He proposes specific solutions. To those who have been seriously concerned about the problem, Justice Meyer's proposals seem reasonable and attainable.

At the outset, Justice Meyer recognizes that *legal* sanctions must be applied. He maintains that codes of ethics will be no more effective in this area than they are in any area of human relations. Though the press's freedom of speech, he says, "must be accorded the widest range compatible with the essential requirement of fair and orderly administration of justice, such freedom is not an absolute." Accordingly, Justice Meyer concludes that we need a legislative statute, delaying publication of certain specific kinds of information which could be prejudicial.

This statute would establish a new misdemeanor. Trial by jury and the right of appeal would be provided for any person indicted under it, and specific punishment would be applied to those found guilty.

Justice Meyer's statute would bind jurors to secrecy, "just as grand jurors are now bound." It would prohibit "not only attorneys and prosecutors but also any employee of an attorney or of the district attorney's office or of the police department or the courts from making any public statement, or directly or indirectly furnishing to any news media any information the publication of which would be prohibited under this statute."

When a case comes before the press at a preliminary hearing publication of all evidence introduced . . . should be *delayed* until it is admitted at trial. News accounts about such a hearing could recount the nature of the charge, the decision of the court, and descriptive material concerning the hearing itself, but not evidence or expression of opinion concerning guilt or innocence. . . . Unless rules of evidence are to be rendered wholly meaningless, delay in the publication of such material is essential.

Justice Meyer then defines the kind of information whose publication he would delay, and divides it into two sections. In the first section, he places

publication of the fact that a confession had been made, or of prior criminal record of an accused, at any time prior to the admission in evidence of the confession or criminal record or to the rendition of the jury's verdict. . . . Evidence of unsworn statements of material fact or which relate to character or credibility cannot under our rules of evidence be presented to the jury during trial, and presentation through the newspaper should be prevented . . . until after the verdict is rendered. . . . Expressions of opinion, whether through man in the street polls, columnists' comments or editorials concerning the effect of evidence introduced, the credibility of witnesses or the guilt of the accused, usurp the function of the jury, and since available scientific evidence indicates that the expressions of opinion by press and commentators have a strong persuasive effect, they should likewise be included.

Other types of information about the crime fall into the second section. Publication of this information would not necessarily constitute an offense, unless a jury found that such publication "created a serious and imminent danger of substantial prejudice." Items in this section would include "interviews with the family of a victim of a crime, statements that a witness will testify to particular facts, publication of the names and addresses of jurors sitting in the case, matter which appeals to racial, political, economic, or other bias."

Most importantly, if a publisher is brought to trial for this misdemeanor, the jury should *not* be required to find that the publisher acted with intent to prejudice.

(This part of Justice Meyer's recommendations is, apparently, in reaction to a U.S. Supreme Court decision which stated that in a libel suit brought against a newspaper, proof of the libel itself is not enough to win the case. The aggrieved party must also prove that the newspaper intended the libel maliciously. This decision, obviously, grants great freedom to newspapers, since it is very nearly impossible to prove intent. Thus if this Supreme Court decision were to be applied to Justice Meyer's proposed misdemeanor statute, the statute would have very little strength.)

The Justice's proposal also says, " . . . nor should the truth of the published material be a defense, since it is the right to a trial free of the unfairness of prejudice that the statute is designed to preserve."

Simply, this means, for example, that if a newspaper publishes, before trial, the prior criminal record of a defendant, the publishing of that record is prejudicial to that defendant. If the newspaper were then to be brought to court under the new statute, the publisher could not plead that, since the criminal record actually existed, printing it did no harm.

Withal, Justice Meyer is not unaware of the vital need for a free press. This need, he says, requires that *his proposed statute not prevent publication of material any longer than is essential to preserve the fairness of the trial.*

Thus, publication of the items listed in the two sections would be proscribed beginning at the:

moment the crime is committed . . . until jury trial is waived, or, if the case is tried before a jury, until the material is actually admitted in evidence, or, if it is never admitted in evidence, until the jury renders its verdict.

If there were a related case pending [still] untried, such material dealing with the case first tried as would prejudice trial of the related case would not be released for publication at the conclusion of the first trial, but would be released at the conclusion of the pending trial.

Where a retrial is ordered, either on motion or as a result of an appeal, the proscription would . . . be reimposed as soon as the retrial was ordered. If a long time elapsed before such an order, the danger from publicity released at the end of the original trial would be remote. If the elapsed time is short, reliance would have to be placed upon the power of the court to grant a continuance, unsatisfactory though that solution may be.

Justice Meyer, with great vehemence, concludes: "The proper balance between freedom of the press and the right to a fair and impartial trial will not be achieved except by the adoption of a statute and rule such as proposed."

Justice Meyer obviously does not want to take freedom from the press. Nor does anyone else. Justice Meyer's sole objective, as is the objective of this book, is to safeguard the right to due process of law. His proposal would not abridge the freedom of the press to publish what it wants to publish. It would not interfere with the public's "right to know." It would do nothing more than restrain the press from printing prejudicial information until such time as that information could no longer prejudice.

To reasonable men, that would be justice.